MW00874538

Hand-Print And Heart-Print Memorials

Stones of Remembrance

by
Verna-Lea Turner

*"Bless the Lord, all His works
(including every part of this book!),
in all places of His dominion. Bless the Lord, O my
soul!"*
—Psalm 103:22

Bloomington, IN Milton Keynes, UK

authorHOUSE®

AuthorHouse™
1663 Liberty Drive, Suite 200
Bloomington, IN 47403
www.authorhouse.com
Phone: 1-800-839-8640

AuthorHouse™ *UK Ltd.*
500 Avebury Boulevard
Central Milton Keynes, MK9 2BE
www.authorhouse.co.uk
Phone: 08001974150

All scripture quotations, unless othrwise indicated, are taken from the New King James Version®. Copyright© 1982 by Thomas Nelson, Inc. Used by permission. All rights reserved.

©*2007 Verna-Lea Turner. All rights reserved.*

No part of this book may be reproduced, stored in a retrieval system, or transmitted by any means without the written permission of the author.

First published by AuthorHouse   4/4/2007

ISBN: 978-1-4259-4860-3 (e)
ISBN: 978-1-4259-4789-7 (sc)
ISBN: 978-1-4259-4788-0 (hc)

Library of Congress Control Number: 2006906774

Printed in the United States of America
Bloomington, Indiana

This book is printed on acid-free paper.

ACKNOWLEDGMENTS:

To Juanita Essert who advised, edited and re-edited material, encouraged and endured the recorder;

To Anita Hashim who read and edited, researched appropriate Scriptures, and kept insisting that God be glorified in all details;

To Mary (Connie) Bryant for help with graphics;

To Vondia Caruso for researching Scriptures;

To Mark Chambers at Young Life for editing and giving technical advice;

To Beverly Chambers for editing and encouraging the recorder;

To the Prayer Group for praying;

To Timothy Fitch for production help;

To Carol Tenhet who prayed and prophesied, "If you do your best, God will do the rest!"

Thank you and may God "showcase" you in heaven for your help!

DEDICATION

I dedicate this book to two groups of people:

1) to each one who participated in the book project by providing his or her testimony, thus in two years time, providing a course in Christianity 101 for the recorder, and
2) to my parents, grandparents, and their ancestors, some of whom came to America with the Moravians and told their descendents the story of Jesus.

We will not hide them from their children,
Telling to the generation to come
the praises of the Lord,
And His strength and His
wonderful works that He has done.
For He established a testimony
in Jacob,
And appointed a law in Israel,
Which He commanded our
fathers,
That they should make them
known to their children;
That the generation to come
might know them,
The children who would be born,
That they may arise and declare
them to their children,
That they may set their hope in
God."
-- Psalm 78:1-7

"I neglect God
…for the noise of a fly,
for the rattling of a coach,
for the creaking of a door."
-John Donne

CONTENTS

"Now all these things happened unto
them for examples; and they are written
for our admonition,
upon whom the ends of the world are come."
--1 Corinthians 10:11

"For whatever things were written before
were written for our learning, that we
through the patience and comfort of the
Scriptures might have hope."
—Romans 15:4

"Stones Of Remembrance"

According to a report from a Young Life Conference, only thirty percent of America's young people brought up in Christian homes remain in church. That means the Church and, possibly, God's Kingdom lose seventy percent of our youth! The research shows that young people (influenced by what they see and hear on television and movies) do not believe what Christian parents and the church teach them. **They have little or no fear of God.**

Disturbed by the report, I sat in amazement one evening as our family lingered around the dinner table listening to an uncle recount some of his Korean War experiences, especially the time, when **alone** on night-watch on a ship in pitch-black darkness, two hands suddenly and supernaturally came from behind, rested forcefully on his shoulders, and kept him from falling 60 feet to his death! "Looking around, I saw no one, only the uncovered death-trap hatch," he stated. "How many people know of your near-death experience?" I queried. "Not too many;" he replied, "I usually don't talk about my war experiences."

In talking to friends and family about healing adventures, I have asked if their children or grandchildren know of their "God-encounter." Usually, the answer is, "No, I just don't get around to telling them." In my own family, I recall my parents telling of my sister at 3 years of age being healed of mastoiditis--an inflammation of the bone behind the ear. More recently, God healed one friend (given up by doctors to die) of tuberculosis and pernicious anemia; another friend He healed of cancer!

These experiences remind us that several times in the Old Testament God commanded people to leave "stones" of remembrance **so generations to come would not forget what God had done for that generation:**

"Choose twelve men from among the people, one from each tribe, and tell them to take up twelve stones from the middle of the Jordan from right where the priests stood and to carry them over with you and put them down at the place where you stay tonight." So Joshua called together the twelve men he had appointed from the Israelites, one from each tribe, and said to them, "Go over before the ark of the Lord your God into the middle of the Jordan. Each of you is to take up a stone on his shoulder, according to the number of the tribes

of the Israelites, to serve as a sign among you. In the future, when your children ask you, 'What do these stones mean?' tell them that the flow of the Jordan was cut off before the ark of the covenant of the Lord. When it crossed the Jordan, the waters of the Jordan were cut off. **These stones are to be a memorial to the people of Israel forever.***" (Joshua 4:2-7)*

Repeatedly, God worked marvelous wonders! However, the people did exactly as many do today. They forgot, turned their backs, and their children and the following generation knew nothing about God's actions and interventions. (Historically, a day of God's power--or great revival--lasts, on the average, for about 40 years and changes only the generation experiencing the touch.)* A pattern of the following nature occurs: Moral decay sets in; someone cries out to God for revival; God answers and society is changed for awhile; then the cycle repeats.

"They would not listen, however, but persisted in their former practices. Even while these people were worshiping the Lord, they were serving their idols. To this day their children and grandchildren continue to do as their fathers did, 2 Kings 17:40-41. When our fathers were in Egypt, they gave no thought to your miracles; they did not remember your many kindnesses, and they rebelled by the sea, the Red Sea,...Psalm 106:7;... because you have ignored the law of your God, I also will ignore your children, Hosea 4:6."

HAND-PRINT AND HEART-PRINT MEMORIALS is the recorder's attempt to leave a chronicle for future generations of the unexpected and miraculous dealings of God in the lives of some of our spiritual leaders--both in the church world and in the "market place." I wanted the testimonies to be different, to have a personal touch.

A few years ago, when my mother was Clerk of the Court, El Paso County, Colorado Springs, Colorado, I sometimes visited the court house and enjoyed perusing old hand-written documents. Each time I saw **her** writing or name on a document, I became extremely interested. It was as though a part of **her spirit** resided in the handwriting! A dream began forming to collect handwritten

----
* *The Cure Of All Evils,* Mary Relfe, Ph.D.

3

testimonies of some of our spiritual leaders and to develop the project *Hand-Print And Heart-Print Memorials*.

Sending letters to possible respondents, I asked for **a handwritten** account of some special way God had dealt with them—handwritten because the writing of a person is very personal and unique, just as the Father's dealing with the heart of each of us is unique and special. For **future generations to have a record of both impressions** was my goal. (I also asked for biographical information and then permission to tell their story.)

Because I requested the "encounter" be told in each person's own handwriting, a book of this type was difficult to compile. Sometimes people eagerly said they had an experience to relate but then changed their mind when they asked, "Are you sure you want the story in cursive writing?" "People won't be able to read my writing," or "My writing is so bad." People such as Dr. Ruth Swope, Joy Dawson, and my mentors Juanita Essert and Anita Hashim reminded me that the *message* is the most important part; others encouraged the project to go forward saying, "May God bring **your vision** to fulfillment. It is a worthy and needed one."

Since the 20th Century, most correspondence has been typewritten or computer-generated. In a study done at Yale University (**Handwriting In America**) by Tamara Thornton, the author calls handwriting "a lost art." "**Not only do we lose the art but we lose seeing the very soul of a person**!" We have lost a record of something that is very personal: namely, the handwriting and signature that register uniqueness about each of us--just as unique as our footsteps or fingerprints.

Dr. John C. Maxwell has a letter handwritten and signed by John Wesley from 1791. He says he prizes it. "When you see the thoughts of someone you respect written in his or her own hand, it really means something." **A handwritten note communicates that you care.**

Dr. Les Parrott, founder of the Center for a Relationship Development, tells of recent research into the topic of authenticity. When a word of encouragement is written down for another person, "it is often **perceived to be more genuine** than when it is spoken," leaving little doubt about the value of a handwritten note (*25 Ways To Win With People*).

From historical archives we have the cursive handwriting of Oral Roberts, Charles Spurgeon, Mother Teresa, and a few other spiritual leaders. Now I am adding other people of faith to the historical collection and am indebted to those who have contributed their God-encounters.

By using the handwritten word in the stories included in this book, we have a record of the special dealings of God in each life—**stones of remembrance**—and we have an authenticated mental picture generated by the handwriting--something a computer cannot do.

As a last point, not the most important, not the most intellectual, not even the most convincing, but a strong point from the Scripture: The Apostle Paul **realized the importance of his own writing as a way to convince someone else of the reliability of a note. (Perhaps somewhat trivial, but the** *Scripture* **records it!):**

"I, Paul, am writing this with my own hand. I will repay—not to mention to you that you owe me even your own self besides."
--Philemon 2:19

"I, Paul, write this greeting in my own hand, which is the distinguishing mark in all my letters. This is how I write."
--2 Thessalonians 3:17

A TYPED VERSION FOLLOWS EACH HANDWRITTEN ACCOUNT.

THE BOOK IS NOT DESIGNED TO BE READ IN ONE SITTING; we would encourage you to take your time to absorb what God has done for some people in our generation! "Stones often are not noticed until they are needed."

Perhaps, in the future, some of the young people from our generation who have forgotten to fear God will **discover** the book,

read about someone's encounter with a loving God, **learn** how someone else responded to life, **know** that there were people of great faith in our generation, **be drawn** to follow His commandments, and **return** His love! That is the desire of the recorder.

Handwriting convinces others about your identity!

Testimony convinces others about God's reality!

"He [God] is a person, not a philosophy or concept. We must whet the appetites of the people of God for more of the supernatural. *Testimony has the ability to stir up that kind of hunger.*"—Bill Johnson

"I call heaven and earth as witnesses today
against you, that
I have set before you life and death, blessing and
cursing;
therefore choose life, that both you and your
descendants may live;
that you may love the Lord your God,
that you may obey His voice,
and that you may cling to Him,
for He is your life
and the length of your days;
and that you may dwell in the land
which the Lord swore to your fathers,
to Abraham,
Isaac, and Jacob, to give them."
—Deuteronomy 30:19-20

I clicked on Google on the Internet and asked the question, Why Do We Sing? Surprisingly, within a short time the reply came back. John Bell, Scottish composer and hymn writer, said, "We sing because we can."

We sing because we can! Astounding! Other species may warble or howl or bray or tweet, but God made mankind with the capacity to sing, and we sing for no particular reason other than it may make us feel good or it is fun.

Some researchers have suggested the following benefits of singing:

1. People who sing tend to live longer than people who do not.
2. Singing helps people learn mnemonic devices (melody, rhythm, rhyme, imagery). thus making it easier to memorize.
3. Singing helps people feel like an accepted member of a group.
4. People sing because it helps them experience worship.

The apostle Paul seems to suggest that rather than being drunk on wine be "high" on making music in our heart to the Lord. (Singing cures depression, monotony, and tension.) *"And do not be drunk with wine...but be filled with the Spirit, speaking to one another in psalms and hymns and spiritual songs, singing and making melody in your heart to the Lord."*—Ephesians 5:18-19

Dr. Jack Hayford states that *"When breathed upon by the Holy Spirit, and born upon the lips of devotion in praise"* singing becomes an "explosive force." He says singing is "the climate in which God Himself works"—*"Who laid its [earth's] cornerstone, when the* **morning stars sang together** *and all the sons of God shouted for joy?"*—Job 38: 6-7

Through singing God delivers us from "the soul's dark night" and brings hope and deliverance.—*("Where is God my Maker, who gives* **songs** *in the night,"*…. Job 35:10)

Through singing God often protects us from our enemy.—
(*You are my hiding place; You shall preserve me from trouble; You shall surround me with **songs of deliverance**.*
—Psalm 32:7)

Through singing and the ministry of the Word we encourage each other.—*(Let the **Word** of Christ dwell in you richly in all wisdom, teaching and admonishing one another in psalms and hymns and spiritual songs, **singing** with grace in your hearts to the Lord."—Colossians 3:16)*

Through singing God conquers the enemy when we are outnumbered.—*(Now when they began to **sing** and to praise, the Lord set ambushes against the people...."*
—2 Chronicles 20:22)

In a forward to his book, Martin Luther once wrote*: "Next to the Word of God, the noble art of music is the greatest treasure in the world. It controls our thoughts, minds, hearts, and spirits...."*

Our next participants portray the joy our generation found in gathering together—to sing!

9

MR. JAMALL BADRY

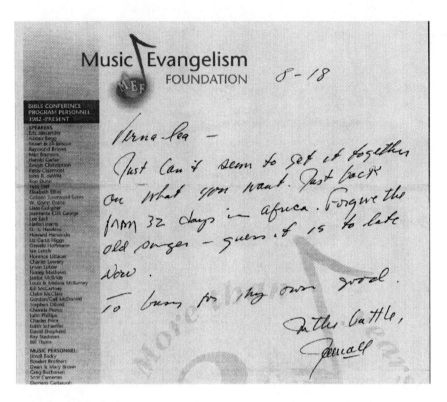

Music Evangelism
FOUNDATION   8-18

BIBLE CONFERENCE
PROGRAM PERSONNEL
1982-PRESENT

SPEAKERS
Eric Alexander
Alistair Begg
Stuart & Jill Briscoe
Raymond Brown
Mac Brunson
Harold Carter
Evelyn Christenson
Patsy Clairmont
John R. deWitt
Ron Dunn
Tony Evans
Elisabeth Elliot
Colleen Townsend Evans
W. Glyn Evans
Liam Goligher
Jeannette Clift George
Lou East
Harlan Harris
O. S. Hawkins
Howard Hendricks
Liz Curtis Higgs
Oswald Hoffmann
Ian Leitch
Florence Littauer
Charles Lowery
Erwin Lutzer
Tommy Mathews
Janice McBride
Louis & Melissa McBurney
Bill McCartney
Clebe McClary
Gordon/Gail McDonald
Stephen Olford
Chonda Pierce
John Phillips
Charles Price
Edith Schaeffer
David Shepherd
Ray Stedman
Bill Thom

MUSIC PERSONNEL:
Jimell Badry
Rawker Brothers
Dean & Mary Brown
Greg Buchanan
Scot Cameron
Damaris Carbaugh

Verna-Lea —
Just can't seem to get it together
on what you want. Just back
from 32 days in Africa. Forgive the
old singer — guess it is too late
now.
To busy for my own good.
                    In the battle,
                         Jamall

Busy, on the move, "in the battle," Jamall Badry often refers to himself as "the old singer." An evangelist, recording artist, world traveler for the cause of Jesus Christ are more appropriate titles. He is also the founder of the Music Evangelism Association that gathers annually for one week in June in Colorado Springs, CO., attracting people from all over the world. The list of musicians and speakers is imposing and matchless in earthly and heavenly terms, for an anointing exists that bathes one for fourteen services in Scripture and worship-filled music. Yes, this is happening in my generation!

THEY "DO MORE WITH LITTLE"

One of my greatest spiritual experiences took place in the African country of Zambia. We had been ministering to those wonderful, very poor people for over three weeks. I had not only been teaching, but singing for Crusades in the bush country.

The last Sunday we drove at least 25 miles into the "bush" where lions used to roam. Finally, after an eternity of driving we arrived at one of the churches in an area where I had sung many times.

The church was absolutely packed, with no room for us to walk in except the front. The music man had trained three choirs. The kids' choir sang, then the young people's choir, and then 18 adults walked to the front to sing their number. Mind you, the church had no music whatsoever, no piano, guitar, organ, or even drums. Somehow the man in charge of music had secured a pitch pipe. He kept looking at me while he tried to get the choir on pitch with the pitch pipe. No music, no instruments, no paper, pencils, nothing!

Finally, he gave the downbeat, and to my amazement they sang perfectly, Handel's Alleluia! We have choirs in the U. S. who couldn't sing that work if they practiced all year.

All of the American team were stunned and in tears. I jumped up and shouted, "Sing it again!" and with a grin as wide as I've ever seen, the director replied, "We'll sing it for our benediction". Africans do more with little than any people I've been around. They are worthy of our love and respect.

Jamall Badry
October 2004

JAMALL BADRY

"A Man Who Lives By Faith; A Man With A Mission"

There exists in Colorado Springs, Colorado, a well-kept secret, a Conclave that is **not** intended to be hidden! People visit the Colorado Springs area to view or ride the train to the top of 14,110' Pikes Peak, to duck-walk through stalactites at the Cave of the Winds, to photograph the cathedral-shaped rock spires in the Garden of Gods, to experience the three-faith chapel at the Air Force Academy, to climb the 224 steps at the side of the Seven Falls, to egg-walk for balance as they cross the 1,053' high (and over a quarter mile long) suspension bridge hanging over the Royal Gorge, or for a variety of other reasons.

Definitely, it is a tourist city, but it is also a natural military site and spiritual military site, having two bases; one fort; NORAD (The North American Air Defense Command); and The Air Force Academy. The <u>Christian</u> <u>Yellow</u> <u>Pages</u> lists eighty-plus Christian ministries--not churches--headquartered in the vicinity: The Christian Booksellers' Association, Dr. James Dobson's Focus On The Family, Compassion International, Dick Eastman's Every Home For Christ, The Navigators, Young Life, The World Prayer Center, and others. Recent statistics show Colorado Springs to be one of the most conservative cities in the United States. In the past, especially in the summer, Indian tribes gathered in the area. Now, of course, God spends most of His summers here; He brushes no other sky on earth with such white, billowy cumulus clouds!

Also, headquartered in Colorado Springs is the Music Evangelism Foundation, which since 1982, hosts the Music Evangelism Foundation (MEF) Bible Conference. Held the last week in June, the Conference attracts people from **every denomination** across the United States and now from Northern Ireland, England, Mongolia, Canada, and Africa to hear the Word preached by "outstanding" ministers and to worship with "outstanding" musicians from across the world.

During my generation, churches traditionally scheduled at least two revival meetings each year when an evangelist and special singer held services lasting for a week or longer. It was also traditional to have "camp-meetings" or Bible Conferences. Twenty or thirty years ago people arranged their vacations to attend the meetings. Today MEF Bible Conference is one of two remaining in the U.S.; Mr. Jamall Badry, a man with a vision and faith in a mighty God, founded the Music Evangelism Foundation Bible Conference.

Badry grew up in a non-Christian family but was taken to church by neighbors, gave his heart to Christ at six or seven years of age, and developed a love for gospel music. In college he sang with various groups--one time even on the Ed Sullivan TV show. Once a star football player, once a commissioned officer in the U.S. Army, Badry attended the University of Oklahoma, receiving a degree in music, and then spent two years as minister of music at a Baptist Church in Oklahoma City. Sensing God had another call on his life, Badry soon went into full-time music evangelism.

Besides being a recording artist, Jamall Badry has held concerts in all parts of the United States, Canada, England, Scotland, India, and Africa. Desiring to bring unity to the Body of Christ and to share the Gospel of Jesus Christ; he willingly goes to every denomination or civic organization that invites him.

Since Badry first went into full-time music evangelism, he has lived **a life of faith** relying totally on God for all of his needs. After moving to Colorado Springs in 1979, his dream was to host a Bible conference with great preachers and musicians. When asked to explain what a Bible Conference is he said, *"It is a concentrated effort in the study of God's precious Word, accented by soloists, choirs, and great congregational singing. It is not a one-hour worship service as most of us know it."*

Knowing that other people would surely feel the same way, for the First Conference in 1982, Badry rented a **1,400 seat auditorium**, invited Ron Dunn, Bible teacher from Irving, Texas; Harold Carter, a pastor from Baltimore, Md.; Bernhard Kuiper, pastor of Village Seven Presbyterian Church, Colorado Springs, and Dr. Harlan Harris, Colorado evangelist. Also on the program the first night were trombonist Lanny Marshall and soloist Alice Pegues and testimonies by Representative Bob Stephenson, Winston Parker, and businessman, Will Perkins.

The attendance was not impressive, but people exclaimed: "I've never heard preaching like that in my life.' 'Why haven't we done this before?' 'What a blessing'." Badry was not to be discouraged by the attendance.

After the third year, attendance climbed to 700 and Badry was told by a friend, *"Jamall, no one will pay for your vision."* Badry's thought: *"They would if attendance increased... to 700 in a short three years, and if some of the greatest speakers and singers in the world accepted our invitation to attend—which they have.* **But something worse than not paying for someone else's vision is not having a vision at all."**

Within a few years, attendance rose consistently to 2,000. The Conference is always free, causing some critics to say, *"This just won't work."* When people ask Badry why he doesn't charge a fee, his reply is, *"I don't believe anyone should have to pay to hear the Gospel. A price that keeps one person away is a price MEF will not pay."*

Badry's purpose is to "reach out to people everywhere in a greater way with God-given talents." And he does just that. In fact, it is mind-boggling to page through the years' records, see the names of speakers, the names of musicians, and to learn of the out-reaches MEF, through faith in God, has achieved.

Each year "great speakers" from around the world minister the Word; some have been the following:

Elisabeth Elliot, author and former missionary to Ecuador;

Eric Alexander, pastor of St George's Tron Parish Church in Glasgow, Scotland;

Stuart and Jill Briscoe, pastor and author from Waukesha, Wisconsin;

Tony Campolo, sociology chairman at Eastern Baptist College;

James Irwin, astronaut who walked on the moon;

David Shepherd, South Wales evangelist;

Evelyn Christenson, author and speaker;

Ray Stedman, pastor of Peninsula Bible Church in Palo Alto, California;

Oswald Hoffman, speaker for the long-running "Lutheran Hour";

Jeannette Clift George, nationally known speaker and actress who starred in *"TheHiding Place"*;

Edith Schaeffer, author;

Bill McCartney of Promise Keepers;

Liz Curtis Higgs, author;

Florence Littauer, author and speaker;

Chonda Pierce, Christian comedienne;

Charles Price, President of Capernwray Bible School in Lancashire, England;

Erwin Lutzer, best-selling author and featured speaker on The Moody Church Hour;

Johannes van der Colff, founder and director of Revival Challenge in South Africa.

Some of the "famous musicians" have been:

Dean Wilder of the "Hale and Wilder" team;

Vernard Johnson, acclaimed as "The World's Greatest Saxophonist";

Greg Buchanan, world-class harpist from California;

Stacy Blair, blind trumpeter;

Bill Murk, violinist, and Scott Ayers, pianist from Greenville, South Carolina;

Bowker Brothers, piano duet from Canada;

Johnny Hall, a Dove Award nominee from Atlanta, Georgia;

Jubilation Brass, 25-piece brass ensemble from Howard Payne University inBrownwood, Texas;

Dean and Mary Brown, full-time evangelist who host their own weekly TV show;

John Starnes, tenor soloist and recording artist;

Damaris Carbaugh, soloist with the Brooklyn Tabernacle Choir;

Paul and Marj Ferrin, pianist, organist, composers living in Colorado Springs;

Many choirs from across the nation.

Comments such as the following are left each year:

"We were soothed, stirred, challenged, convicted and loved. It was the kind of experience all God's children should have...a bit of heaven on earth."

"One night we stumbled into an MEF meeting and heard from the Word of God what my heart so desperately needed—how to find the way back to God. What a happy journey it has been."

Like any well-run business, MEF has a Board of Directors, and in 1987, after the 6th Annual conference they began an outreach ministry of feeding the poor and needy on Thanksgiving—a long time faith-dream of Jamall Badry's. The first year 130 people were fed; in later years, winter coats and New Testaments were dispersed. The summer of 1991 marked the beginning of MEF's African Ministry for the training of pastors, but that is another story of "A man with a mission, and a man who lives by faith."

Having parents who migrated to the U.S. (his father from Damascus, Syria; his mother of Lebanese descent) from countries derailed of freedom, is perhaps one reason Badry has such great faith and appreciates the United States and the freedom we experience here. In some of the conferences he has given recognition to a military person who has died "so we could hear singing and preaching such as witnessed in this service."

Oh, yes, another well-kept secret exists: ***"The consensus is that there were 14 people at the first MEF Bible Conference,"*** says Badry, ***"but just who those 14 were is a spot of contention."*** Now more than 100 people claim to have been one of those 14!

"For therein is the righteousness of God revealed from faith to faith; as it is written, the just shall live by faith."—Romans 1:17

God is not a man, that He
should repent. Has He said,
and will He not do?
Or has He spoken,
and will He not make it good?"
—Numbers 23:19

DR. DOUG OLDHAM

I HAVE BEEN SINGING MY TESTIMONY FOR FIFTY-THREE YEARS. IT IS SUMMED UP IN THE LYRICS OF FOUR BILL GAITHER SONGS

1. "THE OLD RUGGED CROSS MADE THE DIFFERENCE"

2. "THANK TO CALVARY"

3. "HE TOUCHED ME"

4. "HE GAVE ME SOMETHING WORTH LIVING FOR"

Doug Oldham

ROMANS 8:28

ONE I WROTE 'IVE GOT TO GO ON'

DR. DOUG OLDHAM

Dr. Doug Oldham was the first soloist to sing for the National Religious Broadcasters. He has given more than 5,000 concerts, appeared in Billy Graham crusades, and has been the featured soloist on the Old Time Gospel Hour. He has sung at such places as Carnegie Hall, Wolftrap, The Super Dome, and the White House. Dr. Oldham has sixty-four albums with sales in the millions that have brought him two Dove Awards, two Angel Awards, and a Gold Album for "Alleluia." He attended two music conservatories, and was honored with an honorary Doctor of Divinity. He wrote the book, *I Don't Live Here Anymore.*

Dr. Oldham has sung for Queen Elizabeth and Prince Phillip of England and for five U.S. Presidents—Dwight Eisenhower, Richard Nixon, Gerald Ford, George Bush, Sr., and George W. Bush.

"And we know that all things work together for good to them that love God, to them who are the called according to His purpose."
--Romans 8:28

"Who is the man that fears the Lord?
Him shall He teach in the way He chooses.
He himself shall dwell in prosperity,
and his descendants shall inherit the earth.
The secret of the Lord
is with those who fear Him,
and He will show them His covenant."
--Psalm 25:12-14

"THOSE WHO ARE SENT TO HER!"

*"Oh Jerusalem, Jerusalem, the one who kills the prophets and stones **those who are sent to her!** How often I wanted to gather your children together, as a hen gathers her chicks under her wings, but you were not willing!"*
--Matthew 23:37

"Now as He [Jesus] drew near, He saw the city and wept over it, saying, 'If you had known, even you, especially in this your day, the things that make for your peace! But now they are hidden from your eyes. For days will come upon you when your enemies will build an embankment around you, surround you and close you in on every side, and level you, and your children within you, to the ground and they will not leave in you one stone upon another, because you did not know the time of your visitation'."
--Luke 19:41-44

The following entries are the testimonies and biographical sketches of two teachers of end-time events:

Testimony

convinces

others

about

God's

reality!

DR. RAY M. BRUBAKER

The history of Ray Brubaker, radio and TV commentator for the program, "God's News Behind the News": Fifty years ago I enrolled at Moody Bible Institute in Chicago, and found work at WMBI as a studio assistant — my boss was George Beverly Shea. I was promoted to announcer, then given my own program, God's News Behind the News. The day I had to announce the bombing at Hiroshima when nearly 100,000 Japanese died, I felt the call to leave broadcasting for trailer evangelism, and Cathedral Caravan was born!

With my wife, Darlene, for ten years we brought the good news of the Gospel to trailer parks, fairs, wherever the place where people could gather and listen and come to know Christ as Savior and Lord. But lifting the heavy canopy that opened the caravan, I found my arm and shoulder seriously affected. Dr. Fierbach, rated third in the nation among joint and bone surgeons, operated, during which time a part of fluid burst forth. Afterward he told my wife I would never have use of that arm. However, I felt led to go to prayer and fasting. On the 4th night I was awakened to hear the Lord say, "I've healed you." Reporting to the doctor, he called all his assistants to see what he may have done to bring about my healed condition, but to God gave the glory, for He healed me. How marvelous!

Then I felt the call of God leading me to return to broadcasting. Soon God's News Behind the News was on the air again, and before long 1300 stations gave us "free" time! How marvelous!

Another incident comes to mind. Sponsored by 100 Chicago churches, we parked our Caravan near the headquarters for the nomination of President Eisenhower. How thrilling it was to hear Gov. McKeldin of Maryland, nominate Ike, reading from our setup on which was printed II Chronicles 7:14 "If my people — shall pray and seek my face — " Later, it was President Eisenhower who beat on to put the words, "under God," in our pledge of allegiance. How marvelous!

Ray M. Brubaker

The history of Ray Brubaker, radio and TV Commentator for the program, "God's News Behind the News":

Sixty years ago I enrolled at Moody Bible Institute in Chicago, and found work at WMBI as a studio assistant—my boss was George Beverly Shea. I was promoted to announcer, then given my own program, God's News Behind the News. The day I had to announce the bombing at Hiroshima when nearly 100,000 Japanese died, I felt the call to leave broadcasting for trailer evangelism, and Cathedral Caravan was born!

With my wife, Darlene, for ten years we brought the good news of the Gospel to trailer parks, fairs, wherever the places where people could gather and listen and come to know Christ as Savior and Lord. But lifting the heavy canopy that opened the caravan, I found my arm and shoulder seriously affected. Dr. Lienbach, rated third in the nation among joint and bone surgeons, operated, during which time a pint of fluid burst forth. Afterward he told my wife I would never have use of that arm. However, I felt led to go to prayer and fasting. On the 4th night I was awakened to hear the Lord say, "I've healed you." Reporting to the doctor, he called all his assistants to see what he may have done to bring about my healed condition, but to God goes the glory, for He healed me. How marvelous!

Then I felt the call of God leading me to return to broadcasting. Soon God's News Behind the News was on the air again, and before long 1,200 stations gave us "free" time! How marvelous!

Another incident comes to mind. Sponsored by 100 Chicago churches, we parked our Caravan near the headquarters for the nomination of President Eisenhower. How thrilling it was to hear Gov. McKeldin, of Maryland, nominate Ike, reading from our notepads on which was printed II Chronicle 7:14 "If my people…shall pray and seek My face…." Later, it was President Eisenhower who went on to put the words, "under God," in our pledge of allegiance. How marvelous!

Ray M. Brubaker

Dr. Ray Brubaker

"The man whose message is needed now more than ever."

"*...Whosoever shall confess Me before men, him shall the Son of man also confess before the angels of God.*"--Luke 12:8

As a five-year-old boy, Dr. Brubaker's mother led him "**to invite Jesus to save him**." Since that time many years ago, he has been mightily used by God to persuade many thousands **to invite Jesus to save them**.

Serving as a bridge of hope for our generation, Dr. Brubaker links what is going on in our world with what God proclaims in the Holy Scripture. He has been a part of American history as a pastor, as an evangelist, and as a news commentator with his own program, broadcasting GOD'S NEWS BEHIND THE NEWS on over 1,200 radio stations, six television networks, and an association of TV stations across the country.

Shaken by the events occurring in 1945 where 140,000 died in Hiroshima and where 80,000 were killed in Nagasaki (He said temperatures at the center of the blast reached an estimated 5,400 degrees), Dr. Brubaker put together five caravans in the United States and a "caravanette" in Japan. For ten years, they "crisscrossed" the U. S. and Japan using films such as THE ATOMIC BOMB warning people, "Be Ye Ready! Jesus is coming soon!"

Through the years, Brubaker's concern deepened for people to be awakened for the return of Christ. In the 1960's while pastoring a church, he awakened "following a vision or dream in which various persons appeared crying out, '*Why didn't you warn us; why didn't you tell us of this awful day,*' referring to the Rapture in which they were left behind." After spending hours in prayer, he promised God that, as did John the Baptist, he would be faithful to warn people "to flee the wrath to come." Dr. Brubaker believes as a Church "we have assumed that our readiness for rapture depends solely upon our being saved." He questions that to be the case when Jesus admonished "believers to be ready for the Lord's return." Now he sees the possibility of a terrorist act "of such dimension that the Lord could use the occasion to rapture the saints just before such a strike occurs."

Dr. Brubaker received his formal training at Moody Bible Institute. With a God-inspired interest in broadcasting, be became a scholar doing volumes of research for the papers he writes and for GOD'S NEWS BEHIND THE NEWS. To emphasize "the scriptural aspect of readiness...for the return of Christ," he ends nearly every broadcast with this warning: "Be ye therefore ready also; for the Son of man cometh at an hour when ye think not"—(Luke 12:39-49).

His writings and messages are filled with detailed research and corroboration by other Biblical scholars. For example, he quotes Rev. Billy Graham as saying, *"There is a shallowness, a surface-like quality to much of our Christianity today in America that cannot possibly delight the heart of God."* Graham noted concerning the parable of the foolish virgins (Matthew 25:1-10), *"Outwardly they were identical. They were the same to the eye but not in the heart.... Five of them had an inward supply of oil and five of them did not. There are thousands of professing Christians whose relationship to Christ is all external. They serve Christ with their lips but their hearts are far from Him."* To this type of "Christian," Brubaker addresses his message.

Dr. Brubaker initiated THE INTERNATIONAL PROPHECY CONFERENCE that is held each year. He also has written several books, including <u>UFO's</u> <u>in</u> <u>the</u> <u>Bible</u>; <u>The</u> <u>Purpose</u> <u>of</u> <u>the</u> <u>Great</u> <u>Tribulation</u>; and <u>Rapture,</u> <u>A</u> <u>Reward</u> <u>for</u> <u>Readiness</u>. In addition to researching, reporting, and writing books, he served as President of the St. Petersburg Theological Seminary in Florida.

Dr. Brubaker and his wife of the past few years (since the passing of his first wife) live in Ohio. Minnie, who once was Billy Graham's secretary and also sang in the King's Karollers Quartet on SONGS IN THE NIGHT, now helps Dr. Brubaker with his staff and ministry.

With world events occurring as rapidly and with the Rapture believed to be very close, Dr. Brubaker "believes Luke 17:29-30 may explain how the rapture may occur:"

*"But the same day that Lot went out of Sodom it rained fire and brimstone from heaven and destroyed them all. **Even thus** shall it be when the Son of man is revealed."* Brubaker says, "Nuclear destruction could mark Christ's Coming!" And Jesus warned, *"Take*

heed to yourselves, lest at any time your hearts be overcharged with surfeiting and drunkenness, and cares of this life, and so that day come upon you unawares. For as a snare shall it come on all them that dwell upon the face of the whole earth. Watch ye therefore and pray always, that ye may be accounted worthy to escape all these things that shall come to pass, and to stand before the Son of man."—Luke 21:34-36

Our generation has been blessed to have a leader who is willing to step forward and say, **What if**—

What if, many Christians are shallow?

What if, it does take holiness to see the Lord? (Hebrews 12:14— *"Follow peace with all men, and holiness, without which no man shall see the Lord;..."*)

What if, instead of millions missing, millions will be left behind?

What if, Revelations 7:13-14 refers to those who have been left behind?(*Sir,...."These are they which came out of great tribulation, and have washed their robes, and made them white in the blood of the Lamb."*)

What if, Christ is returning for those who are watching and looking for His return? (Hebrews 9:28—"*...and unto them that **look** for him shall He appear the second time...."*)

"...Whosoever shall confess Me before men, him shall the Son of man also confess before the angels of God."—Luke 12:8

"Hear this, you elders, and give ear, all you inhabitants of the land! Has anything like this happened in your days, or even in the days of your fathers? Tell your children about it, let your children tell their children, and their children another generation."

—Joel 1:2-3

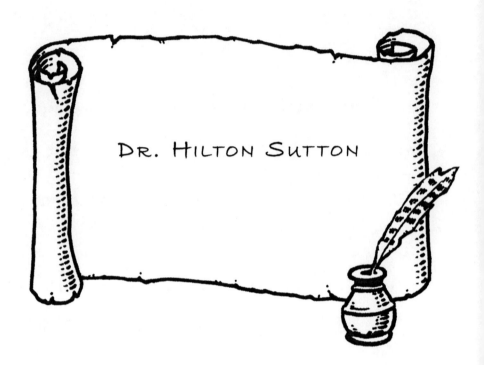

DR. HILTON SUTTON

May 4, 2004

Dear Verna-Lea,

Thank you for the invitation to participate in your book. I believe it to be a God idea.

Two divine revelations changed my life's direction and ministry. First, prior to accepting the call of God into the ministry of His Son; I discovered a special Holy Spirit anointing that I knew I must experience. As a born again Christian, church soloist and choir director I knew the anointing of the Holy Spirit but it was not to be compared with the one that came upon the minister when he stepped into the pulpit to minister the word of God. My desire for that anointing was ever increasing and a major reason for accepting God's call into the ministry of His Son. I was not and am not disappointed.

Secondly, through my years of studying the Holy Scripture, I amazingly discovered that Bible prophecy was not a doom, gloom or fear filled message from our heavenly Father. The seventeen prophetic books of the Bible are just like the other forty nine; filled with faith, hope and love.

2434 Roman Forest Blvd. • PO Box 1259 • New Caney, TX 77357
Office: 281-689-1260 • FAX: 281-689-1265
www.hilton-sutton.org • e-mail: hsm@hilton-sutton.org

HILTON SUTTON

WORLD MINISTRIES

I am abundantly blessed serving in the ministry of my Lord Jesus.

Hilton Sutton, Th.D.

35

Thank you for the invitation to participate in your book. I believe it to be a God idea.

Two Divine Revelations changed my life's direction and ministry. First, prior to accepting the Call of God into the Ministry of His Son, I discovered a special Holy Spirit anointing that I knew I must experience. As a born again Christian, church soloist and choir director I knew the anointing of the Holy Spirit. But it was not to be compared with the one that came upon the minister when he stepped into the pulpit to minister the Word of God. My desire for that anointing was ever increasing and a major reason for accepting God's call into the ministry of His Son. I was not and am not disappointed.

Secondly, through my years of studying the Holy Scripture, I amazingly discovered that Bible prophecy was not a doom, gloom or fear-filled message from our Heavenly Father. The seventeen prophetic books of the Bible are just like the other forty-nine, filled with Faith, Hope and Love.

I am abundantly blessed serving in the ministry of my Lord Jesus.

Hilton Sutton, Th.D

DR. HILTON SUTTON

At eighty-five years of age, Caleb asked Joshua for the city promised him by God forty-five years earlier (Deuteronomy 1:36), *"Give me this mountain (Hebron) [requested Caleb] and Joshua blessed him and gave Caleb the mountain"* (Joshua 14:12).

Similarly, at a time when other men might be asking for the price of an Alaskan cruise or the price of a new fishing pole, Dr. Hilton Sutton is asking God for the money to purchase a **Pilatus Aircraft.** The Pilatus is an "SUV" of planes with a turbo prop engine. This plane would enable Dr. Sutton to fly across the U.S. at 310 miles per hour with only one stop, allowing more time and energy to preach the gospel in **all** parts of the world!

For fifty-seven years Dr. Sutton has brought to **our generation** a gospel of hope, of really good news with emphasis on preparing the body of Christ to be "Caught up to meet the Lord in the air," (1 Thessalonians 4:16-18); of teaching about end-time "seasons;" of stirring Christians to witness about Christ in preparation for the end-time harvest; and of understanding the Book of Revelation.

Often referred to as the "senior prophetic teacher of our day," Dr. Sutton preaches not of "doom and gloom," but of hope and expectation as he teaches us to win others and to look forward to the soon return of Christ. *"Lukewarm Christians will be left behind"* (Matthew 25:1-13 and Revelation 2:1-7 and 3:14-22), so God mandated him in 2004 to start teaching around the world. He warns, *"Don't allow yourself the ordeal of coming back to the Lord as a Tribulation saint."*

To understand the "seasons" is important. Dr. Sutton stresses that it is preposterous to set dates, but we can know the season, and we are now in the "season" of Jesus' appearance. When asked, "When is Jesus coming?" he says we do not know the day or hour but **we have a clue**. *"This important clue is found in the teachings of Jesus recorded in Matthew 24:44-47. Here is the clue: 'Blessed is that servant whom his master, when he comes, will find him so doing.' Doing what? Simply **learning how to get along with fellow Christians and in <u>unity</u> winning the lost to Jesus.**"*

In his book *Revelation Revealed*, prodding us to win souls, Dr. Sutton reminds us that God's throne room (as revealed in the Book of

Revelation) is large enough to house all of the righteous at one time plus one hundred billion angels—in one room—all in bodily form! Each day we should ask God to send someone across our path with whom we may share the Gospel; in fact, he reminds us that we cannot "be a born-again follower of Jesus and not be a soul winner." Quoting John 16:8, *"And when he [the Comforter] is come, he will reprove the world of sin..."* Dr. Sutton says, **"therefore, *there isn't a person alive who isn't presently under Holy Spirit conviction."*** (Each person still has a free choice, but it is not the will of God that any one be lost.) Sutton tells us to begin with our families. He still sits down with some of his family members and says to them, *"I want to tell you, until you folks get back in church and serve God as you know you should, nothing's going to work right in your life. You need to get in the house of God and serve Him with all your heart, then things will get straightened out."* **This hour is the soul-winning season.**

As a young person, Dr. Sutton had difficulty with the teaching that people were dying and going into eternity without having heard about Jesus. One day while studying God's Book, he realized that his lack of knowledge of the Word of God had created his dilemma. God directed him to Titus 2:11-15: "***For the grace of God that brings salvation has appeared to all men*....**" To our generation and for people who commonly use the same dilemma to make excuses for not believing in God or for not accepting Jesus Christ, Sutton's response is straight-forward: *"I discovered from the authority of the Word of God that it is utterly impossible for anyone to be born into this world and not have, at some time or another in their life, an opportunity to come to know God's Son, Jesus Christ—utterly impossible."* He reminds us that even the heavens declare the glory of God as Roman 1:20 states: *"For the invisible things of him from the creation of the world are clearly seen..., **so that they are without excuse.**"*

Dr. Sutton earned his Th.D. from Jerusalem Cornerstone University and Seminary and served as a youth pastor, a music director, and as senior pastor before God called him to full time prophecy teaching. He is on radio and television throughout the United States and various parts of the world. Recently his programs were linked so that 90% of Israeli homes have access to his broadcast. He is the author of more than fifteen books including *Revelation Revealed, The Next Resurrection,* and *The Antichrist.* His fourteen-hour study of the Book of Revelation is offered as a course (on campus or by correspondence) for certificate credit at Oral Roberts' University. His positive, Bible-based messages have brought thousands to salvation and "set believers free from unscriptural fear of the future."

A man of great energy, an intellectual, and a student of the Bible, Sutton is also a man of great conviction. If the Bible says it, we do not need to argue; we do not need to run from one conference to another; "don't compromise; don't lose your first love." He is also a man with a sense of humor: he refers to many as "pew potatoes," and challenges a congregation with the question, *"Why hasn't Jesus already come back?"* (the title of a book on which he is currently working). His answer: *"Come back tomorrow night and I will tell you!"*

Presently, Dr. Sutton and his wife, Joanne, who often travels with him, live in Roman Forest, Texas. He is chairman of the Board of Hilton Sutton World Ministries, with offices in New Caney, Texas. He is a member of the Executive Board of World Ministry Fellowship of Dallas, Texas, and was a founding trustee of the International Charismatic Bible Ministries of Tulsa, Oklahoma. He is also an active member of the International Convention of Faith Ministries of Little Rock, Arkansas.

Much in demand as a speaker, Dr. Sutton has addressed the Joint Chiefs of Staff of the United States Military, the Israeli Knesset, and the Israeli Foreign Ministry. He is acquainted with past Israeli Prime Minister Benjamin Netanyahu, and his personal friends include past Israeli Prime Ministers Shimon Peres, Yitzak Shamir, the late Yitzak Rabin, and Menachem Begin.

Dr. Sutton says he has lived to see many great "waves" or movements of God (the great "tent" healing meetings, the Jesus movement, the Word movement, etc.) but he declares, ***"There is currently another wave of the Holy Spirit beginning to build."*** **We are in the wave of the "End-time Harvest," and** *"souls are the object of this wave of the Holy Spirit."* He believes we are a "marked generation," an age that will *"culminate with the appearance of Jesus to catch His church away,"* and we are here to witness *"the greatest hour of the fulfillment of Bible prophecy in all of history!"*

"My people are destroyed
for lack of knowledge. Because
you have rejected knowledge,
I also will reject you
from being priest for Me;
because you have forgotten the law
of your God,
I also will forget your children."
--Hosea 4:6

"God 'Dwells' In Our Praises"

"But thou art holy, O thou that inhabits the praises of Israel."|
—Psalm 22:3

"I started singing that great hymn, 'A Mighty Fortress Is Our God.' I sang 'Jesus Loves Me,' Bible choruses, and every Christian song I could remember. I was no longer conscious of the cold, only of Jesus. With eyes closed, my head barely touching the wall (He could not sit or stand in a pitch-black, cold room because of the cold), *I whistled, sang, even imitated a trumpet blasting out praises to the Lord. Although I didn't think through the many Scriptures that* support it, **I had entered the highest level of warfare against the enemy—praise. Psalm 22:3 says that God inhabits our praises.*** *I don't know how this is accomplished, but it's true. The mighty Deliverer, the Messiah, the Savior was with me. He held my shaking body in His arms. I was with Jesus, no matter what happened."*
—Tom White—U.S. Director for The Voice of the Martyrs

As Tom White was distributing Gospel literature over Cuba (He had already successfully distributed more than 400,000 pieces), his small plane crash-landed on a Cuban highway. Arrested by Communists and put in solitary confinement, he was sentenced to 24 years in a Cuban prison. Spending seventeen months in jail, he was released in 1980 after many appeals from U.S. Congressmen and even Mother Teresa.

William Law, an **Eighteenth Century** English clergyman, taught his generation that the shortest and best way to happiness and perfection was *"to make it a rule to yourself to thank and praise God for everything that happens to you. For it is certain that whatever seeming calamity happens to you, **if you thank and praise God for it, you turn it into a blessing....**"*

During the second half of the **Nineteenth Century**, England's most loved preacher, Charles Spurgeon, said we should *"Cry for grace from God to be able to see God's hand in every trial, and then for grace...to submit at once to it. Not only to submit, but to acquiesce, and to rejoice in it...**I think there is generally an end to troubles when we get to that**."*

Our next participant tells of an encounter with God that eventually led him to an understanding and application of praise and thankfulness in his own life. Then he brought this message to our generation.

*The word "inhabit" (Hebrew *yawshab*) means "to sit down, to remain, to settle, or marry." Praise enthrones God to deal directly with our enemies (Psalm 149—*"Let the high praises of God be in their mouth...to execute vengeance on nations.... This honor have all His saints. Praise the Lord!").*

Handwriting

convinces

others

about

your

identity!

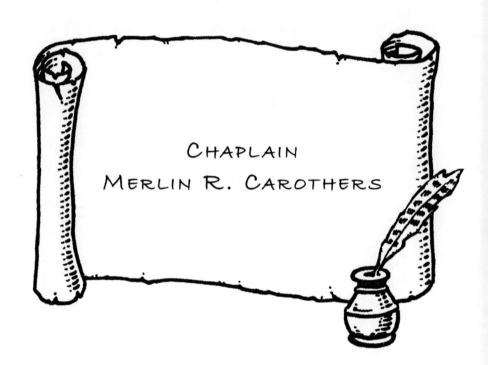

CHAPLAIN
MERLIN R. CAROTHERS

In my spirit I heard, "Merlin, are you glad that Jesus died for your sins? Does it make you feel good to think of His dying for your sins?"

"Yes, Lord, it really does."

"Does it make you feel happy to know that He gives you eternal life by His death for you? It makes you glad that they took My son and drove nails into His hands and feet?"

These questions were strange and ones I had never heard or thought about. I finally had to say, "Yes, Lord, it does. I don't understand it, Father, but I am glad."

To my relief I heard, "Yes, son, I want you to be glad. And for the rest of your life I want you to be just as glad when anything happens to you that is any less difficult than what they did to My son."

It was easy for me to say, "Yes Lord, I will," but I had no idea where God's directions were going to lead me. — Merlin R Carothers

45

MERLIN R. CAROTHERS

www.FoundationofPraise.com
Monthly newsletter: "Praise News"

In my spirit I heard, "Merlin, are you glad that Jesus died for your sins? Does it make you feel good to think of His dying for your sins?"

"Yes, Lord, it really does."

"Does it make you feel happy to know that He gives you eternal life by His death for you? It makes you glad that they took My Son and drove nails into His hands and feet?"

These questions were strange and ones I had never heard or thought about. I finally had to say, "Yes, Lord, it does. I don't understand it, Father, but I am glad."

To my relief I heard, "Yes, son, I want you to be glad. And for the rest of your life I want you to be just as glad when anything happens to you that is any less difficult than what they did to My Son."

It was easy for me to say, "Yes, Lord, I will," but I had no idea where God's directions were going to lead me.

—Merlin R. Carothers

P.O. Box 2518
Escondido, CA 92033

CHAPLAIN (LTC) MERLIN R. CAROTHERS
"A Man on The Run"

"Rejoice always, pray without ceasing, in everything give thanks; for this is the will of God in Christ Jesus for you."
—I Thessalonians 5:16-18

Thankful for everything that happens to you? That is the message God gave Chaplain Merlin Carothers for our generation! He will be remembered for the message of *"learning to praise God at all times in every situation."*

Since first printed in 1970, *Prison to Praise* has sold over 17 million copies. Even though the book is about any bondage ("a prison of circumstances") a person may experience, it shows how to be set free. To penitentiaries all over the world, the book has been sent and millions say *"it has changed their lives and introduced them to the solution to their problems."* A "most unusual book," with a message that some will not accept until a seemingly hopeless situation occurs, it went into its 91st printing in 2003. Thirteen other books (translated into 56 languages) have followed, many of which continue to recount stories and lessons learned about living a victorious life through learning to rejoice and praise God for everything. Carothers has shared the praise message in *"forty-nine states and dozens of foreign countries."*

To live and praise God in dark and unpleasant circumstances, one's perspective on life must totally change. Chaplain Carothers says that a person *"learns to know the joy of abiding in Jesus Christ, and everything else in his life becomes secondary."* He learns to *"Rejoice evermore, pray without ceasing, in everything give thanks; for this is the will of God in Christ Jesus for you."* —I Thessalonians 5:16-18

The verse is a command that, if obeyed, produces happiness and joy in a person and Chaplain Carothers continues to bring that message to our generation.

A counseling session with Carothers might go something like this: (An Army wife married to an alcoholic husband comes to see Chaplain Carothers, convinced that her problem has but one solution. She tells of the ordeals she has endured for years. In final desperation the wife decides to take the children and leave; however, friends persuade her to talk to the Chaplain first.)

"Whatever you say, Chaplain, don't tell me to stay with him," she said. *"I just can't do it."* *"I don't really care whether you stay with him or not,"* the Chaplain says. *"I just want you to* **thank God that your husband is like he is.***"* He explains to her what the Bible has to say about thanking God for everything, and if she tried it, God would be released to solve the problem. She thinks he is ridiculous but agrees to kneel while he prays for *"God to release in her enough faith to believe that He is a God of love and power who holds the universe in His hand."* She decides to believe God and thank Him for her husband's condition. Two weeks later the wife calls saying that a miracle has occurred; the husband is not drinking and he now spends time with his family. Carothers relates many stories such as this in his books.

Chaplain Carothers' early life began rather tragically. Bitter at God after his father's early death, 12-year-old Carothers "became a rebel at heart." After working his way through school in Ellwood City, Pennsylvania, but not having enough money to finish college, he wanted to "join the action in WWII." To "find excitement," Merlin volunteered for the Airborne Division training at Fort Benning, Georgia, and after earning the honor of "wearing the glistening jump boots," he wanted more excitement and volunteered for training as a demolition expert. Waiting to be sent overseas, but not having enough excitement while waiting, he and a buddy went AWOL, stole a car, and planned to commit a robbery that was foiled; however, a six-state alarm had gone out and they were picked up by the FBI. Sentenced to five years in the Federal Penitentiary, the judge temporarily suspended the sentence for Carothers to return to the army and be sent overseas.

In Europe, Carothers served not only as a demolition expert, but became a Master Parachutist (90 jumps) in the 82nd Airborne Division during three major campaigns of World War II. At the close of the war, he attained the honor of serving as a personal guard to General Dwight D. Eisenhower. He also achieved the dubious honor of becoming involved in black marketeering (buying cartons of cigarettes for $10 from soldiers and selling them for $100) and found a way to become very rich, bringing suitcases full of money orders home. (We relate this story from his book to show how God later became glorified.)

Back from Germany and visiting his grandparents, Merlin reluctantly attended church one night. It was in that service that a voice behind him said, *"Tonight you must make a decision for Me; if you don't, it will be too late."* At first Merlin inwardly argued with what he knew to be the voice of God, but then "went forward to make public his decision for Christ." That night Merlin Carothers began a new life of running for Christ.

After giving his life to Christ, God dealt with Carothers about the suitcase full of $100 money orders. Eventually they were either flushed down the toilet or went to the Government-backed Conscience Fund. Merlin was poor now, but he was filled with joy. Still to be resolved, however, was the matter of the three years remaining on his sentence. Reporting to the Pittsburgh parole board and district attorney, Merlin found to his amazement that he had received a presidential pardon **signed by President Truman!** The district attorney said it had something to do with his excellent combat record. It was at this time he believed God was calling him to be a minister, so he finished college in 2½ years and then enrolled in Asbury Seminary and completed the 3 year course in two years. He became a Methodist minister.

In 1953, Carothers volunteered for the Army Chaplaincy and re-entered the Army serving in Germany, Korea, the Dominican Republic, Panama, and Vietnam. In 1966, he received orders to go to Vietnam with the 80th General Support Group from Ft. Bragg, and then in 1967 he returned from Vietnam to Ft Benning, Georgia. Just twenty-three years earlier he had left there a handcuffed prisoner but now returned as a chaplain! He had been where the action was but had also witnessed much heartache.

During this period of his life discouragement set in. To find a Biblical solution to his problem he began searching the Scripture for passages pertaining to joy. Verses such as Luke 6:23 stood out: *"When you are hungry...when men shall hate you...rejoice in that day; leap for joy."* He then had the encounter with God that is hand-recorded in this report. He said, *"Yes, Lord. For the rest of my life I am going to be thankful. I'll praise You, I'll rejoice, I'll sing, I'll laugh, I'll shout, I'll be filled with joy for whatever you permit to come into my life."* He made a choice. *"Most gladly therefore will I rather glory in my infirmities, that the power of Christ may rest upon me. Therefore I take pleasure in infirmities, in reproaches, in necessities, in persecutions, in distresses for Christ's sake; for when I am weak, then am I strong."*--II *Corinthians 12:9-10*

A pilot, lecturer, and retired pastor, Merlin and wife Mary live in California where they still minister in churches and on TV and by writing (as a team) a monthly newsletter Praise News which can be ordered from FoundationsofPraise.com. At one point in his life, after serving the Lord for many years, Carothers was eager to retire, to relax, and to enjoy a quiet life, but God reminded him that the Bible does not talk about retirement. His come-out-of-retirement message is told about in *Let Me Entertain You.* Mary Carothers has learned well the message of praise, also, for in a recent newsletter she reiterated: *"When we stand back and praise and thank God for what He is doing (even though we may not see evidence of it) then it releases His hands to work in our lives."* The Foundation of Praise supplies free copies (but requests donations) of **Prison to Praise** to federal, state, and county prisons; to hospitals; to military bases throughout the world; and to Crisis Pregnancy Centers.

A pivotal point occurred in Chaplain Carothers' life after an accident in Korea where he lost 60% of his vision in one eye. The doctors said vision would never return, but he was healed. Desiring to know more about this power, he researched and studied the Word. He came to believe that the secret of the Christian life is found in Colossians 1:27: *"Christ in you. The hope of glory." "Not that we become like Him, or that Christ had been a mere man, an example for us, but that He lives in us and transforms us from within. He lives in us."* Not reliance on hypnosis, or transcendental meditation, or positive thinking (all of which Carothers researched and determined there was danger in opening the mind to these influences), but relying on Christ living within us is the secret of the Christian life. After attending a retreat and asking the Holy Spirit to come into his life and empower him, Chaplain Carothers realized that *"We rely on Jesus Christ because He lives in us and His power operates through us because He is 'the vine and we are the branch'."* We can do nothing in our own power.

After that experience Carothers' life and ministry changed. He was empowered as he prayed for people. He became "obedient to the impressions or urgings" he felt within him, and then he simply trusted God. As long as he relied on Christ in him, "it seemed that God took his days, and every detail, every appointment...." No longer did he experience confusion and conflicts. "Letting go and letting God" freed him to speak the words and message God had for a person or group, and he was able to spend more time in prayer and Bible reading.

Other chaplains would come secretly to his office and ask him to pray for them as he had learned to pray (in another language). Men would often comment at the joy Merlin had, saying, *"It is impossible to have the joy you have."*

At another point in his life, Chaplain Carothers learned the difference between symptoms and healing. Headaches and allergies often had plagued him, and during one of these bouts he *"began to think of how good God was to let me have this infirmity of the flesh. He was permitting me to have it to teach me something. It wasn't an accident of nature that I was allergic to so many things. God had planned it this way for His glory and for my good. Thank you, Lord, for Your goodness. If You want me to have this I'll just trust You to heal me whenever You want to."*

"What do you want me to do?" God asked him.

Carothers said, *"Heal me, Lord."*

"Heal you or take away the symptoms?"

"Aren't they the same, Lord?"

"No, they are not."

"Okay, Lord, then just heal me and I won't pay any attention to the symptoms."

He knew God had shown him something new. He realized that symptoms mean nothing, that *"Faith in God's promise was all I needed; then satan could fake all the symptoms he wanted."* Soon, however, the Chaplain was tested. Symptoms still evident and suffering from running eyes and nose, one night he walked to the place where he was supposed to preach--without a handkerchief! When the meeting was over, he suddenly was aware that he had no symptoms of hay fever.

One of Chaplain Carothers' books (***The Bible on Praise***) is a compilation of Scriptures on praise and thanks that includes some of the following:

I Thessalonians 5:16-18*:* *"Rejoice always, pray without ceasing, in everything **give thanks**; for this is the will of God in Christ Jesus for you."*

Romans 8:28*:* *"And we know that all things work together for good to those who love God, to those who are the called according to His purpose."*

Philippians 4:6-7*:* *"...but in everything by prayer and supplication with **thanksgiving**, let your requests be made known to God; and the peace of God which surpasses all understanding, will guard your hearts and minds through Christ Jesus."*

Hebrews 13:15*:* *"Therefore by Him let us continually offer the sacrifice of **praise** to God continually, that is, the fruit of our lips, giving **thanks** to His name."*

Ephesians 5:20*:* *"...giving **thanks** always for all things to God the Father in the name of our Lord Jesus Christ,...."*

Psalm 50:23*:* *"Whoever offers **praise** glorifies Me."*

Psalm 113:3*:* *"From the rising of the sun to its going down the Lord's name is to be **praised**."*

Psalm 66:8*:* *"O, Bless our God, you peoples! And make the voice of His **praise** to be heard...."*

Luke 6:23*:* *"When you are hungry...when men shall hate you... rejoice in that day; leap for joy."*

Habakkuk 3:17-19*:* *"Though the fig tree may not blossom, nor fruit be on the vines;...yet I will **rejoice** in the Lord, I will joy in the God of my salvation."*

Isaiah 55:8-11*:* *"'For My thoughts are not your thoughts, nor are your ways My ways', says the Lord....So are My ways higher than your ways, and My thoughts than your thoughts...."*

Genesis 45:5, 8*:* *"But now, do not therefore be grieved or angry with yourselves because you sold me here; for God sent me before* *you to preserve life.... So now it was not you who sent me here, but God;...."* (God meant it for good!)

"Miracles, power, and victory will all be a part of what God does in our lives when we learn to rejoice in all things."—(even the street light turning red, or trusting God to lead us to the right mechanic for car repair)—When we really believe that, the power of God is released in our lives.

One powerful statement Chaplain Carothers makes about his discovery regarding praise is found in ***Power in Praise***. He has had time to ponder the questions people ask him; he has had time to research more Scriptures dealing with praise; he has had more time to apply the command to praise God and rejoice, and he says:

"I have come to believe that the prayer of praise is the highest form of communion with God, and one that always releases a great deal of power into our lives. Praising Him is not something we do because we feel good; rather it is an act of obedience. Often the prayer of praise is done in sheer teeth-gritting willpower; yet when we persist in it, somehow the power of God is released into us and into the situation. At first in a trickle perhaps, but later in a growing stream that finally floods us and washes away the old hurts and scars."

What relief a person experiences when he learns to thank God for every situation. We don't do this to manipulate God or to expect Him to give a solution we want. In fact, for awhile, things may seem to go awry! But we enter into a rest knowing that God loves us and that He is now released to work so that things work for our good.

To the troubled Carothers would say: *"God has you exactly where He wants you. He could have interfered when you made a wrong choice. If we trust and praise Him, He makes even our wrong choices work for good. Praise Him for your circumstance. God will change them if this is His design. Very often it is our attitudes that hinder the solution of a problem. But His perfect plan is to bring each of us into fellowship and communion with Him and so He allows circumstances and incidents which will bring our wrong attitudes to our attention."*

To those troubled about mistakes or sins of the past: *"Don't think of your past as a chain around your neck. Thank God for every detail of your life and believe He has permitted all of these things in order to bring you to the place where you are now."*

To those who lack faith: *"Our viewpoint makes all the difference. God loves you and does everything He can to bring you to Him. Ask God to increase your faith; choose to believe.* (In 75% of the letters Chaplain Carothers receives, people tell of choosing to praise God and about marvelous results; in 25% of the letters people say they are unable to praise God and believe He is at work, and thus, they remain defeated and discouaged.)

When bad things happen: *"Accept the fact that God is the all-powerful God He says He is, and that nothing happens without His knowledge or permission. Sometimes God chooses to use apparently evil circumstances to bring about His plan of good. We express our faith by praising Him. Stephen knew that, although his persecutors meant evil against him, God meant it for good."*

To those worried about the future: *"I want you to tell everyone who will listen to be thankful for every detail of their lives, and I will open the windows of heaven and pour out more blessings—free and undeserved--than they can ever ask or hope for."*

To those crying to God to make a change: *"Praise God for everything in our lives instead of pleading with Him to change the circumstances that displease us, for power is released when we do so."*

If you are inclined to grumble or complain: *"Praise God for the situation, even for having to get out of bed of a morning."*

If you have no joy: *"Ask God for joy, make a decision to love others, and begin rejoicing in all things." "These things I have spoken to you, that My joy may remain in you, and that your joy may be full. This is My commandment, that you **love** one another just as I have loved you (John 15:11-12)."*

"If I was a nightingale
I would sing
like a nightingale,
if a swan, like a swan.
But since I am a rational
creature, my role is to
praise God."

— Epictetus

It occurred approximately 2,700 years ago and approximately 2,000 years ago; it occurred in 1914; so why not again in our age?

Supernatural interruptions have often surprised people; in fact, they sort of make people nervous, and newspapers or television reports may shy away from such stories. Acts 12 relates such a story when Peter was imprisoned:

> (While the church prayed) Peter was placed under heavy guard shackled to two soldiers. *"Suddenly there was an angel at his side and light flooding the room. The angel shook Peter and got him up.... The handcuffs fell off his wrists. The angel said, 'Get dressed. Put on your shoes.' Peter did it. Then, 'Grab your coat and let's get out of here.' Peter followed him, but didn't believe it was really an angel—he thought he was dreaming.*
>
> *"Past the first guard and then the second, they came to the iron gate that led into the city. It swung open before them on its own, and they were out on the street, free as the breeze. At the first intersection the angel left him, going his own way. That's when Peter realized it was no dream..."*
>
> *"Still shaking his head, amazed, he went to Mary's house, the Mary who was John Mark's mother. The house was packed with praying friends. When he knocked on the door to the courtyard, a young woman named Rhoda came to see who it was. But when she recognized his voice—Peter's voice!—she was so excited and eager to tell everyone Peter was there that she forgot to open the door and left him standing in the street.*
>
> "But they wouldn't believe her, dismissing her, dismissing her report. 'You're crazy,' they said. She stuck by her story....All this time poor Peter was standing out in the street, knocking away.
>
> *"Finally they opened up and saw him—and went wild!"*....
> THE MESSAGE—The Bible in Contemporary Language,

Eugene H. Peterson, NAVPRESS, Colorado Springs, Colorado.

2 Kings 6:14-17 records the following theurgy or supernatural account:

> When the king of Aram wanted to capture Elisha the prophet,
> *"he dispatched horses and chariots, an impressive fighting
> force. They came by night and surrounded the city.*
> *"Early in the morning a servant of the Holy Man got up and
> went out. Surprise! Horses and chariots surrounding the
> city! The young man exclaimed, 'Oh, master! What shall
> we do?'*
> *"He said, 'Don't worry about it—there are more on our side
> than on their side.'*
> *"Then Elisha prayed, 'O God, open his eyes and let him
> see.'*
> *"The eyes of the young man were opened and he saw. A
> wonder! The whole mountainside [was] full of horses
> and chariots of fire (angels) surrounding Elisha!"—THE
> MESSAGE.*

More recently, in 1914, an angelic encounter occurred saving the British Army. Reported in the <u>London Evening News</u>, the story (dubbed the "Angels of Mons") was so popular that a waltz "Riders in the Sky" was written on the theme. The article told how the British Expeditionary Force (BEF), outnumbered by three to one by German forces, was saved by "heavenly reinforcements." The Angel, or Angels, suddenly stood between the British and the Germans, causing the enemy to fall back in confusion!

The battle took place on August 26, 1914. In a sworn statement by a British officer, he said that *"while our company was in retreat from Mons, a unit of German cavalry came rapidly after us. We made for a place where the company might stand and fight—but the Germans got there first."* Expecting almost certain death, the British turned and saw to their astonishment a troop of angels between the enemy and them! *"The German horses were terrified and stampeded in all directions."* A lieutenant colonel described how, during the retreat, his battalion was "escorted for 20 minutes by a squadron of 'phantom cavalry'."

From the German side came an account that their men refused to charge a point where the British line was broken because of the presence of a large number of troops. According to Allied records, there was not a single British soldier in the area. THE ENCYCLOPAEDIA OF THE UNEXPLAINED edited by Richard Cavendish (McGraw-Hill Book Co.)

We had planned to stop with these accounts until we read Lt. Carey Cash's book *A Table In The Presence*-- a book of numerous stories of "God's footprints" and God's dealing in individual lives during the war in Iraq. He includes the account of *"how the men of an entire battalion found God in the presence of their enemies."* Lt. Cash, a chaplain to the U.S. Marines, recounts an unusual angelic intervention during April 2003:

"Major Steve Armes, our unit's operations officer and third-in-command of the battalion, said that during the worst part of the fight, he remembered looking up at an overpass just ahead of him and saw that it was lined with AAVs [Amphibious Assault Vehicles equipped with heavy machine-guns] from end to end, like a steel wall. But something caught his attention that made him take a second look: the AAVs were not marked. Whereas all of our battalion's vehicles had the distinct and clearly visible markings of our unit painted in bold white letters and numbers, the ones Armes saw had nothing painted on them at all. As the operation's officer, he of all men in the battalion knew exactly where the various units were positioned and what they looked like.

"But he had no idea to whom those strange AAVs belonged. They were unmarked and out of place, and none of it added up, **except for the fact that their position on the bridge provided a perfect shield from the incoming enemy rounds that were hailing down from surrounding rooftops and balconies.**

"In the heat of battle, Armes simply sloughed it off and kept fighting. But days after the battle he had to think twice. Going back to that same intersection, Armes tried to relocate the overpass on which the strange AAVs had been lined up in a steel column. But he searched to no avail. No matter what direction he looked—north south, east, or west—**the overpass simply wasn't there.**" *A Table In The Presence,* pp. 213-214.

In keeping with the above records, we have included for "stones of remembrance" one more account of angelic activity:

REV. JOE CHAMBERS

Rev Joe R. Chambers
2107 Bel Air St
Taylor, Tx 76574

My Most Significant Encounter with GOD

One Winter mid-night of 1952-53, aboard the aircraft Carrier, USS Valley Forge — off the coast of South Korea, having completed a 12-hour shift in the radio shack, located amidship in "the island," beneath the Captain's bridge. I came down the blacked-out stairway and out onto the flight deck, as I had done every night at this time for several months, to go aft to my quarters.

Our vessel and the other 23 ships of Task Force 77 showed no lights to prevent being a target for Communist shore batteries and submarines.

To get to my quarters, I had to walk in total darkness through spider-like tie-downs that secured the folded-wing aircraft — already prepared for daylight sorties, past "the island, then down onto a catwalk, four feet below the flight deck level.

Having done this night-after-night, I sensed where I was, rather than visually knowing; as I eased along the catwalk, my right hand sliding along the heavy metal rain gutter of the flight deck, my left hand lightly touching the top cable that bordered the walkway,

65 feet above the angry black surging, 40 degree-sea —

Suddenly! I felt two hands grab my shoulders from behind! Instantly, I froze! Every hair on my body stood up! I gripped the cable and rain gutter with all my strength, in the grip of a fear I had never known before. After an "eternal moment," I stretched out my foot in front of me, discovering that an access cover to one of four radio antennas. Always lowered to horizontal during landing operations, had been left open. One more step, and I would have fallen into the near-freezing sea! I would not have been missed for 12 hours, noon the next day.

Carefully, I replaced the hinged cover, then "catwalked" to each of the other three antenna covers — all were in place, THANK GOD! Thirty or forty steps further, I ducked into the hatchway to my living space.

Sleep did not come easily; as I lay there in the darkness — no living soul aware of what I had experienced, GOD's SPIRIT revealed to me that my life was truly in HIS hands —

And, that HE had a very special purpose

for my life, yet to be revealed: to husband a Godly wife, father three Children of our own, be the surrogate father of two others, and to give my life to Kingdom-service as an Under-Shepherd; all despite the fact of an overwhelmingly poor self-image that kept me from seeing myself doing/being what I recognized and admired in spiritual leaders. I am still troubled by that sense of inadequacy, 51 years later— despite the "fruit" of my life across these more than 60 years of being His servant. "It's not about me... it's all about HIM!"

Humbly,

Joe Chambers

born July 4, 1932, LINDRITH, N.M.
Public education: Cleburne, Tx & Carrollton, Tx
BS & Post graduate TEXAS A&M University. Educ, Journ, ENG
Married Georgetta Stolcbarger, 9-8-51
U.S. NAVY 50-54
TEACHER, Freshman English 62-63 Sherman Tx
Middle School Asst Principal and Director of Public Relations 63-67
Boy Scout Professional 1967-1980
Minister of Christian Education/Administration, First Southern Bapt 80-86
Colorado Bapt Gen Convention staff 1986-97,
Director of Ponderosa Retreat and Conference Center
Retired July 1, 1997
Presently: itinerant "missionary" and encourager.

My Most Significant
Encounter With God

One winter mid-night of 1952-53, aboard the air craft carrier, USS Valley Forge—off the coast of South Korea, having completed a 12-hour shift in the radio shack, located amidship in "the island," beneath the captain's bridge, I came down the blacked-out stairway and out onto the flight deck, as I had done every night at this time for several months, to go aft to my quarters.

Our vessel and the other 23 ships of Task Force 77 showed no lights to prevent being a target for Communist shore batteries and submarines.

To get to my quarters, I had to walk in total darkness through spider-like tie-downs that secured the folded-wing aircraft—already prepared for daylight sorties, past "the island," then down onto a catwalk, four feet below the flight deck level.

Having done this night-after-night, I sensed where I was, rather than visually knowing; as I eased along the catwalk, my right hand sliding along the heavy metal rain gutter of the flight deck, my left hand lightly touching the top cable that bordered the walkway, 65 feet above the angry black surging, 40 degree sea—

Suddenly! I felt two hands grab my shoulders from behind! Instantly, I froze! Every hair on my body stood up! I gripped the cable and rain gutter with all my strength, in the grip of a fear I had never known before. After an "eternal moment," I stretched out my foot in front of me, discovering that an access cover to one of four radio antennas, always lowered to horizontal during landing operations, had been left open. One more step, and I would have fallen into the near-freezing sea! I would not have been missed for 12 hours, noon the next day.

Carefully, I replaced the hinged cover, then "catwalked" to each of the other three antenna covers—all were in place, THANK GOD! Thirty or forty steps further, I ducked into the hatchway to my living space.

Sleep did not come easily; as I lay there in the darkness—no living soul aware of what I had experienced, GOD'S Spirit revealed to me that my life was truly in HIS hands—

And, that He had a very special purpose for my life, yet to be revealed: to husband a Godly wife, father three children of our own, be the surrogate father of two others, and to give my life to Kingdom-service as an Under-Shepherd; all despite the fact of an overwhelmingly poor self-image that kept me from seeing myself doing/being what I recognized and admired in spiritual leaders. I am still troubled by that sense of inadequacy, 51 years later—despite the "fruit" of my life across these more than 60 years of being His servant. "It's not about me…it's all about HIM!"

Humbly,
Joe Chambers

"For He shall give His angels charge over you, to keep you in all your ways. In their hands they shall bear you up, lest you dash your foot against a stone."—Psalm 91:11-12

REV. JOE CHAMBERS

"Pure and undefiled religion before God and the Father is this: to visit orphans and widows in their trouble, and to keep oneself unspotted from the world."-- James 1:27

Rev. Joe Chambers referred to himself as an "Under-Shepherd," but Rev. Chambers is not of inferior or of deficient quality (as the dictionary defines that phrase). Dwight L. Moody said, "The measure of a man is not how many servants he has but how many men he serves." For our generation, Joe represents a true Christian with the heart of a shepherd, with a willingness to serve God. An ancestor, the famous Oswald Chambers, said God puts His people where they will glorify Him and Joe Chambers and his wife Georgetta go where God sends them.

I first became acquainted with Rev. Chambers in a hospital room where my mother lay dying. Day and night for several days, he would quietly enter the room, say little in conversation but reassure me that he was there. And so we would sit quietly. Later I was to learn more about him and his gentle Shepherd ways.

In the natural, talented and educated to be a teacher and educator, principal, director of public relations, pastor and director of Colorado Baptist Conference Center until his 1997 retirement, Rev. Chambers and his wife Georgetta are now "itinerant 'missionaries' and encouragers". They literally crisscross the country to bring healing and encouragement to others. Recently he told a pastor (who was on the verge of having pneumonia and had been told by his doctor to stay in bed), "I will make your pastoral calls until you recuperate."

In 2003, Rev. Chambers told of his encounter with a family of a young man who, returning from the war in Iraq, was greeted with divorce papers by his wife who had decided she was in love with another man. The grief-stricken young man committed suicide. Joe Chambers was called to conduct the funeral service. Traveling hundreds of miles, he was met with a "Martin-McCoy" situation.

Brothers of the victim were loaded with guns to kill the girl and her family. Rev. Chambers became the mediator and before the funeral was held, eleven family members accepted Christ, forgave each other, and stowed away their guns.

Commenting on the spiritual condition of some Christians, Charles Spurgeon once said, "*All feeding and no working makes men spiritual dyspeptics. Be idle, careless, with nothing to live for, nothing to care for, no sinner to pray for, no backslider to lead back to the cross, no trembler to encourage, no little child to tell of a Savior, no gray-headed man to enlighten in the things of God, no object, in fact, to live for; and who wonders you begin to groan, and to murmur, and to look within, until you are ready to die of despair.*" Rev. Joe and Georgetta Chambers will never be spiritual "dyspeptics"!

"One generation shall praise Your works to another, and shall declare Your mighty acts."
--Psalm 145:4

"THE GREAT OF THE KINGDOM"...

have been those who loved God more than others did."--A.W. Tozier

*"You [Jesus] put the desire in my heart to spend hours alone with You, **which ruined me for the ordinary.** I knew You were as You are, but You are so much more!"—Joy Dawson*

*"The fear of the Lord is defined as **hating evil and standing in awe of God's holiness and greatness**."--Joy Dawson*

The fear of the Lord is the beginning of wisdom, and knowledge of the Holy One is understanding. For through me your days will be many, and years will be added to your life. If you are wise, your wisdom will reward you; if you are a mocker, you alone will suffer.

--Proverbs 9:10

Mrs. Joy Dawson

Mrs. Joy Dawson

The greatest experience of my life has been pursuing my goals: knowing God intimately to make Him known, and by becoming conformed into Christ's image through submission to the Holy Spirit. It has included seeking God's face daily with intensity of purpose, listening to His voice in order to obey Him instantly, joyfully and wholly.

The Holy Spirit directed me from Jeremiah 9:23,24 to study the character and ways of God from the Bible by getting a large notebook with alphabetical tabs from A to Z. As I daily read the scriptures and came across anything that related to those subjects, I made headings for them in my notebook and then wrote out the accompanying verses. As I meditated on their meaning and applied the truths to my life, it powerfully contributed to fulfilling my goals.

Along with the pursuit of studying every aspect of God's multi-faceted character, the most life changing study of God's ways came from discovering the fear of the Lord. I noticed God has a lot to say about it, and it is defined as hating evil, and standing in awe of God's holiness and greatness. My life was dramatically affected by applying every aspect of this key subject to every area of my life. It brought a passion for holiness in thought, word and action; an essential requirement for intimate friendship with God.

God also revealed to me the importance of being an intercessor — one who stands in the gap between man and God and prays as directed and energized by the Holy Spirit for others. By waiting on God, and allowing the Holy Spirit time to share His heart and His mind with me concerning the object of my prayers brought rapid spiritual growth and helped to fulfill my goal for Christ-likeness.

Another priority was a God-given burden for lost souls to be converted and discipled. This resulted in being involved in many and varied forms of evangelism, internationally. But more importantly, personally, as a way of life, I identify with Jesus' words in Luke 17:10 "... when you have done all these things which you are commanded, say, "We are unprofitable servants, we have done what it was our duty to do." To God be the glory. Joy Dawson

9429 Cordero Avenue, Tujunga, California 91042 U.S.A. • Phone (818) 352-3070 • FAX (818) 352-0990

The greatest experience of my life has been pursuing my goals: knowing God intimately to make Him known, and by becoming conformed into Christ's image through submission to the Holy Spirit. It has included seeking God's face daily with intensity of purpose, listening to His voice in order to obey Him instantly, joyfully and wholly.

The Holy Spirit directed me from Jeremiah 9:23-24 to study the character and ways of God from the Bible by getting a large notebook with alphabetical tabs from A-Z. As I daily read the Scriptures and came across anything that related to those subjects, I made headings for them in my notebook and then wrote out the accompanying verses. As I meditated on their meaning and applied the truths to my life, it powerfully contributed to fulfilling my goals.

Along with the pursuit of studying every aspect of God's multi-faceted character, the most life changing study of God's ways came from discovering the fear of the Lord. I noticed God has a lot to say about it, and it is defined as hating evil and standing in awe of God's holiness and greatness. My life was dramatically affected by applying every aspect of this key subject to every area of my life. It brought a passion for holiness in thought, word and action, an essential requirement for intimate friendship with God.

God also revealed to me the importance of being an intercessor— one who stands in the gap between man and God and prays as directed and energized by the Holy Spirit for others. Waiting on God and allowing the Holy Spirit time to share His heart and His mind with me concerning the object of my prayers brought rapid spiritual growth and helped to fulfill my goal for Christ-likeness.

Another priority was a God-given burden for lost souls to be converted and discipled. This resulted in being involved in many and varied forms of evangelism, internationally…but more importantly, personally, as a way of life.

I identify with Jesus' words in Luke 17:10 "…*when you have done all these things which you are commanded, say, 'We are unprofitable servants; we have done what it was our duty to do'.*" To God be the glory.

Joy Dawson

Mrs. Joy Dawson

SHE DID IT GOD'S WAY!

The common thread, as one writer said, running through all people greatly used by God is one thing: an intense love and hunger for God. **Mrs. Joy Dawson has** that intense love and hunger for God, and she **has** been greatly used by God!

Mrs. Dawson discovered the truth of Ecclesiastes 7:18, *"He who fears God shall come forth from them all."* She says, *"God now puts His authority on us, and He gives us the privileges and responsibilities in His Kingdom that He will not give to those who do not have it [the fear of God]."* *"Fear God and keep His commandments, for this is the whole duty of man"*—(Ecclesiastes 12:13).

As a young housewife, Joy began spending hours in prayer, Bible study, personal and collective evangelism, and **being a servant** to many ministries and especially to spiritual leaders as they spoke to a "house group" from the Dawson's home in New Zealand.

In 1971, Mrs. Dawson and her family left New Zealand coming to the United States as unsalaried missionaries for Youth With A Mission (Y.W.A.M.). She did not seek worldly fame; she did not seek power; she did not seek fortunes; but in her pursuit of God, **she became "the invited speaker"!** God took her throughout the world giving her many things this world seeks—but on a more satisfying level. **He** sent her to the world to teach and to demonstrate what a life of friendship with God can really mean. Since 1970, she has traveled and taught the Bible internationally and at numerous spiritual leadership conferences in fifty-five nations and in every continent. Literally, God brought her "forth from them all" and gave great honor to her because she "feared, not to obey"!

Besides having a worldwide teaching ministry, Joy Dawson is the author of six books, including *Forever Ruined for the Ordinary; Intimate Friendship with God; Intercession, Thrilling and Fulfilling; Some of the Ways of God in Healing; Influencing Children to Become World Changers;* and her latest, *Life Changing Purposes Of The Fire of God.* In addition, she has contributed to four Bibles: *The Spirit-Filled Life Bible, The Women of Destiny*

Bible, Christian Growth Study Bible, and ***The New Spirit-Filled Life Bible.*** Teaching extensively on television and radio, she has seen countless lives touched through the worldwide distribution of her audio and videotapes and books. One unsaved man announced to his wife as she returned home that he had given his heart to Christ; *"I wanted to experience friendship and fulfillment with God as He (God) was described on those tapes."* (He had listened while the wife was at church!)

Often teaching at the first Y.W.A.M International School in Switzerland, Mrs. Dawson once received a note from a minister who had attended the classes. He said, *"What you taught has brought such peace and harmony into our home. We teach our children the fear of God. The fear of the Lord results in all we want our children to learn—total obedience, 100 percent truth, no murmuring or complaining, release from the fear of man and answers in the area of relationships!"* Her teaching brings results!

Joy's parents, John and Grace Manins, were outstanding Christians and soul winners. Her father was an evangelist and Bible teacher. As a result of their influence, at five years of age Joy totally committed her life to Christ. At nine years of age she relates the account of her reaction to her brother telling her about the facts of conception, as their father had just told him. Almost as a **spiritual child prodigy** Joy was filled with awe, and wonder, and worship, and love for God. *"I marveled at His power, His knowledge, and His wisdom that He had worked out a plan as Creator...in order to keep the human race propagated."* This awe of God at nine years of age remains her driving focus!

Mrs. Dawson's book, ***Influencing Children To Become World Changers,*** gives much insight into how to rear Godly children. By example, she and her husband **led** their children. Their children and grandchildren learned to keep a notebook (as Mrs. Dawson had done most of her life) recording the references to the **character and ways of God**, which included recording the scores of times the **fear of God** is mentioned.

From the parents, the descendants learned to ask God regarding small and great matters, and they learned to **wait for an answer**. Five nights every week (after the evening meal) they spent time in sharing

74

portions of God's Word, and then all four of them participated in interceding for other people. To balance the intensity of their "*all-out commitment to know God and to make Him known*," the Dawson's had numerous family picnics, vacations, and activities such as Friday night trips for Chinese food carryout and "*a drive up to the top of a mountain overlooking two harbors in our city.... We wouldn't return home until we had walked or run around the nearby mountain trails, singing crazy songs....*"

One incident demonstrating God's power and care for the Dawson family occurred when 3-year-old grandson Matthew (now a grown man!), disappeared during a car journey on a winter's evening. The parents had stopped at a restaurant, and both thought that Matthew was in the other one's care. When they realized he was missing, a frantic search began. With the parents praying for divine intervention, John's flashlight finally shone on the little boy tucked away in some shrubs. Matthew simply said, "*A man came and touched my shoes and I couldn't do anything but sit down here. I couldn't walk.*" There was no sign of a man and God made it clear to them that Matthew's guardian angel kept him from harm!

To read and hear the teachings of Mrs. Dawson compels one to a new level of irresistible hunger for God. The book *Forever Ruined For The Ordinary*—"the adventure of hearing and obeying God's voice" is an exciting, in-depth book on the subject of Divine Guidance, which has been greatly used of God to bring multitudes into a closer relationship with Him. Of the book *Intimate Friendship With God*, one librarian at the University of Louisiana said if he were stranded on an island, he would want this book and the Bible with him! Mrs. Dawson considers her latest book, *Life Changing Purposes Of The Fire Of God*, the deepest and most challenging of the six books she has written. It is a strong prophetic word to the Body of Christ in which she unfolds nine aspects of the Fire of God, such as the fire of God in testing, the fire of God to purify, and the price for revival fire.

She reminds us that if we are going to be close to God we cannot, because of who God is, escape the heat. ("*Our God is a consuming fire*"—Hebrews 12:29 and "*For everyone will be seasoned with fire*"—Mark 9:49.) When we understand these two truths, life's circumstances will not be as perplexing. It is essential to understand the character of God when we are in the fire: 1. None of our trials have taken Him by surprise; 2. As God allows the difficult circumstances to continue in order to test our reactions to them, He is absolutely just, righteous, and kind; 3. The only sane response to God's "total justice and unfathomable love" is worship and trust.

Mrs. Dawson suggests four ways to pray when we are tested:
1. "Determine in your heart and express it to God that no matter what it costs and how long you're in the fiery trial, you want Him to receive the maximum glory that can come to His wonderful name.
2. "Ask God to use the trial to bring you into a more intimate relationship with Himself and a more passionate love for the Lord Jesus.
3. "Ask Him to reveal to you what He wants to teach you related to any causes and purposes for the fire.
4. "Seek God for direction as to any course of action you are to take, believing Psalm 32:8: 'I will instruct you and teach you in the way you should go; I will guide you with My eye'."

"We either react according to the way God's Word tells us to, and then pass the test, or we react contrary to what the Bible says, and fail the test." And then the test is repeated!

In two of the sections in the ***The Fire Of God,*** Mrs. Dawson reveals some of the depth of the last forty-eight years of her life's study, passion, and prayer burden for worldwide revival and spiritual awakening among the nations. She stresses:

"It's harvest time all over the world.

"God promises personal revival to every life who pursues humility.

"It often takes severe persecution to the Body of Christ for us all to realize how desperately we need each other.

"Unity in the Body of Christ is essential for God's approving presence at all times.

"God commands the blessing when we're united."

Other major purposes of this new book are to help people who are going through deep trials of life to navigate them victoriously, and to help prepare the Body of Christ to become His spotless Bride. Our generation would do well to remember that.

"God in His flawless character, sets up tests basically to see how serious we are in wanting to know Him in order to make Him known.

"God will judge us according to our motives, why we did what we did.

"When we pray frequently for others and never feel the need to tell anyone about it, we know we have passed the test regarding humility and the need for recognition.

"In order for us to pass the timing test, He chooses to show up far later than we would expect or desire.

"Faith does come by hearing the word, but understanding the character and ways of God also reinforces faith.

"The two root sins from which all other sins come are unbelief and pride.

"True brokenness before God and man is a powerful means of releasing the power of the Holy Spirit upon us. –'But on this one will I look [the one who gets God's attention]: on him who is poor and of a contrite spirit, and who trembles at My word'-- (Isaiah 66:2).

"Delayed obedience, partial obedience, and obedience with murmuring is all disobedience according to God's Word.

"I don't know of a state of life that produces hardness of heart like the sin of resentment to those who have wronged us.

"Without fellowship of some kind there's no restoration of relationship. Conversely, forgiveness will always lead to fellowship."

The last chapter "Surviving The Fire Without Being Burned" gives practical advice. In a relaxed manner, after telling about a prolonged physical fire in her own life, Mrs. Dawson encourages others in long-term trials by giving her paraphrase of Daniel 10:1: *"Hang in there, baby, I did speak to you, and one day you'll see the proof of My faithfulness. Remember, I didn't say when I'd show up, but just keep on trusting Me that I surely will!"*

Mrs. Dawson emanates an indescribable and contagious excitement about the close relationship a person can have with God. She teaches and stresses that one must have a fear of the Lord (revere, hate evil, be obedient). She reiterates that knowledge of what God is really like and the fear of the Lord lead to obedience and the two go hand-in-hand. *"The professing Christian without the fear of the Lord becomes the worst advertisement to Christianity, and God has another big disappointment on His hands."*

Many in our generation remember Joy Dawson's teaching on **learning to hear the voice of God**. After teaching sessions, she would have hundreds of people in a large auditorium ask God a question and instruct them to remain silent for at least twenty minutes waiting for a reply. **First,** she taught that all known sin must be confessed in order to have a clean heart (*"If I regard iniquity in my heart, the Lord will not hear"*-- Psalm 66:18*).* Then she taught that a person must ***"die to all human reasoning and desire"* of what we might want the answer to be.** She had us take authority *"over the enemy and silence him in Jesus' name."* (*"Submit therefore to God. Resist the devil and he will flee from you"*--James 4:7.) Finally, we were to *"listen quietly, in expectant faith, for God to speak."* According to the testimonies that followed, **He** certainly did.

On one occasion, Mrs. Dawson spoke in the morning at a spiritual leadership conference on the island of Cyprus and had spent all afternoon seeking God for the message she was scheduled to give in the evening, but God was silent. In the evening, when the leader announced that Mrs. Dawson would bring the message, Joy simply stated that God had not released that understanding to her and, until He did, she had nothing to say!

One hour and ten minutes later, God directed her to two scriptures on waiting on God and told her to share about two other occasions when God severely tested her about waiting on Him. The spiritual leaders not only had a practical lesson of waiting on God but also a demonstration of what it means to be released from the fear of men, through having the fear of the Lord.

Joy emphasizes**,** *"It can cost us many things to fear God and not men—being misunderstood, the loss of friendships, closed doors in ministry, rejection of many kinds, persecution, and even life itself,... but we have no spiritual authority outside obedience to God.... God wants to bring us to the place where **what** He tells us to do is not nearly as important as **who** He is who gives the order.... When Jesus was on earth, the important thing to Him was that the Father had given an order, and it **was the Son's delight to carry it out."***

Even though her obedience to God and the resulting ministry took her away on two occasions from two teenagers and her husband, God rewarded them by both of their children choosing, while in their teens, to become missionaries. One book dedicated to her children John and Jillian whom the mother not only calls her "dearest children" but also her "treasured friends"—reveals the love and respect shared by the Dawson family. Now the Dawson's son John (and wife Julie) is president of Youth With A Mission (an international interdenominational missionary organization operating in 160 nations). Their daughter Jill and her husband John Bills are both leaders and teachers in Y.W.A.M. Mrs. Dawson and her husband Jim (referred to as her "lifelong closest companion") have six grandchildren, four of whom are full-time missionaries with Y.W.A.M.

The Dawson's make their home in California where Joy and her husband are elders of The Church On The Way (Van Nuys, California) and members of America's National Prayer Committee. When she is not traveling, teaching, or writing, Joy's interests are in reading deep spiritual books and sometimes, lately, enjoying decorating and gardening.

Mrs. Dawson knows what God is really like; she fears and has an awe of God; she has learned to listen and to obey; and she draws others to God. What more could one do? In the book *Prayers by Christians Through the Ages*, one of Joy Dawson's prayers is included (along with St. Augustine, Martin Luther, Peter Marshall, and others). The prayer helps us understand the depth of Joy's spiritual relationship with the Father:

"We would be still and know that You are God.... We stand in awe of You..., Your awesome holiness, majestic splendor, blazing glory, limitless power, and unquestionable sovereignty. We worship You for Your flawless character, Your infinite knowledge and wisdom, Your absolute justice, unswerving faithfulness, unending mercy.... We bow our hearts and bend our knees before...Your dazzling beauty, Your fascinating personality, Your incomprehensible humility, Your unsearchable understanding, and Your unfathomable love.... Our greatest need is to have a far greater revelation of what You are really like. We ask You to meet that need."

"How blessed is the man who fears
the Lord, who greatly delights
in His commandments.
His descendants will be
mighty on earth;
the generation of the upright
will be blessed.
Wealth and
riches are in his house,
and his righteousness
endures forever."
—Psalm 112:1-4

STUNNED BY BLESSING FROM GOD!

To live fully surrendered to God often means life is filled with events **announced** by an element of surprise. When one serves Satan, favorable surprises are not the case (Satan may come as an "angel of light" making promises to bring good things, but subtly he brings destruction).

Imagine the first moments of David's surprise as he was called before the Prophet, chosen to become king above his brothers.

Imagine the first moments of Joseph's astonishment to awaken one morning in a palace, placed second in command of a foreign nation.

Imagine Sarah's surprise (she laughed) and Mary's surprise (she pondered events and began to sing) when an angel made the unprecedented announcement that they would give birth.

Imagine Zacharias' initial surprise when an angel announced to him that he and his wife would have a child in their old age (He was frightened and remained speechless for months).

Imagine Isaac's delight when, on an ordinary day, he went to the field to meditate, looked to see "the camels were coming" and saw Rebekah—a love story for all times!

Imagine the first moments of Boaz' surprise to awaken with a woman at his feet--another unequalled love story!

Imagine the first moment of surprise when Esther learns the king has chosen her. Imagine how she felt as the royal crown is placed on her head and she attends the Feast of Esther, a holiday proclaimed in her honor!

In all these encounters, a quiet preparation had been occurring, a grooming, but the **surprises came suddenly**. Until the moment of surprise, the people never would have dreamed of nor imagined God's destiny for their lives.

In a similar manner, a hunger for God and obedience to God produced the surprise events that developed in the lives of the next participants:

"Eye has not seen, nor ear heard, nor have entered into the heart of man the things which God has prepared for those who love Him."
—*1 Corinthians 2:9*

Testimony

convinces

others

about

God's

reality!

JILL AUSTIN

Do You Want A Visitation?
By Jill Austin

Genesis 28:11-12

Then he (Jacob) dreamed, and behold, a
ladder was set up on the earth, and its top reached
to heaven; and there the angels of God were
ascending and descending....

# # # # # #

I want to impart to you a holy jealousy
to have a life-changing visitation with Jesus.
I was ministering in Christchurch, New Zealand
in 1992 at a meeting where the Lord literally came!

I was staying with a pastor and his wife
in an inner city church of about 150 people.
They were a poor crowd but had a desperate hunger
for the Lord.

The Sunday morning meeting was hard
so after the meal I asked the Lord for a
breakthrough for that night.

I saw an open vision of a holy fiery tornado
over the city and I saw myself as a tiny spark
of fire going into this whirlwind of glory.

That night during worship, the atmosphere
began to change - it became saturated with the
tangible glory of the Lord! Many of us could hear

the voices of angels singing with the worship.
I felt that heaven was invading earth!

The crowd had just taken their seats.
As I was asked to come up front and begin,
I felt the Lord behind me and when I looked,
I saw a huge tidal wave of glory as tall as the
ceiling of this old warehouse rolling into the
meeting.

I said, "Lord! What are we supposed to do with
that?" He told me to have the people stand up.
I obeyed and told them what I saw.

As the first tidal wave started to roll into the
room, the Lord said, "This one is for impartation."
As the wave went through the room, the people
were radically gripped by the Lord. Scores of
people went down sovereignly all over the room,
tenderizing hearts and empowering them as His
glory washed over them. Laughter and
weeping erupted throughout the room.

Then I looked behind me and once again
another tidal wave of glory was beginning to
crest. The Lord said, "This one is for deliverance.
Tell them to get up again once more —

Quickly the people responded as another wave crashed over them. People screamed, slithered on the floor like snakes, and were radically delivered from demonic oppression.

A 3rd wave began to roll through the room, the Lord said, "This one is for physical healing!"

Once again the people got up and began to cry out their healings as they were powered & healed by His tangible glory & presence.

Seven waves of glory moved through the warehouse engulfing the crowds in His awesome love.

This took about an hour, so I asked the Lord what I should preach on. He said, "I want you to share on having a child-like heart."

After about 15 minutes of preaching, the heavens opened up and I saw Jacob's ladder come into the middle of the room, with angels ascending and descending.

They were carrying mantles and hot coals of fire. The room became alive with His manifest Presence.

Dozens of people began to dance with invisible partners - His angels. Impartation and the joy of the Lord came. The weighty glory and presence settled into the room - as the very tangible anointing continued to heal bodies, minds and spirits.

Truly heaven had come down and kissed the earth. No one left untouched! Revival broke out in the city. The following weekend over a thousand came as news of this outpouring, this open heavens continued.

For several years thousands and thousands were touched as huge crowds hungered for Jesus - Not only New Zealand - Australia. but many nations throughout the earth from the results of a simple poor group of inner-city people who were desperate and hungry for a visitation.

MASTER POTTER
M I N I S T R I E S

Laguna Hills, CA 92653
www.masterpotter.com

Do You Want A Visitation?
By Jill Austin

"Then he (Jacob) dreamed, and behold, a ladder was set up on the earth, and its top reached to heaven; and there the angels of God were ascending and descending...." Genesis 28:11-12

I want to impart to you a holy jealously to have a life-changing visitation with Jesus. I was ministering in Christchurch, New Zealand in 1992 at a meeting where the Lord literally came!

I was staying with a pastor and his wife in an inner city church of about 150 people. They were a poor crowd but had a desperate hunger for the Lord.

The Sunday morning meeting was hard so after the meal I asked the Lord for a breakthrough for that night.

I saw an open vision of a holy fiery tornado over the city and I saw myself as a tiny spark of fire going in this whirlwind of glory.

That night during worship, the atmosphere began to change—it became saturated with the tangible glory of the Lord! Many of us could hear the voice of angels singing with the worship. I felt that heaven was invading earth!

The crowd had just taken their seats. As I was asked to come up front and begin, I felt the Lord behind me and when I looked, I saw a huge tidal wave of glory as tall as the ceiling of this old warehouse rolling into the meeting.

I said, "Lord! What are we supposed to do with that?" He told me to have the people stand up. I obeyed and told them what I saw.

As the first tidal wave started to roll into the room, the Lord said, "This one is for impartation." As the wave went through the room, the people were radically gripped by the Lord. Scores of people went down sovereignly all over the room, tenderizing hearts and empowering them as His glory washed over them. Laughter and weeping erupted throughout the room.

…..Seven waves of glory moved through the warehouse engulfing the crowds in His awesome love.

This took about an hour, so I asked the Lord what I should preach on. He said, **"I want you to share on having a child-like heart."**

After about 15 minutes of preaching, the heavens opened up and I saw Jacob's ladder come into the middle of the room, with angels ascending and descending. They were carrying mantles and hot coals of fire. The room became alive with His manifest Presence.

…The weighty glory and presence settled into the room as the very tangible anointing continued to heal bodies, minds and spirits.

…Revival broke out in the city. The following weekend over a thousand came as news of this outpouring, this open heavens continued. …For several years thousands and thousands were touched as huge crowds hungered for Jesus—Not only New Zealand—Australia—but many nations throughout the earth from the results of a simple poor group of inner-city people who were desperate and hungry for a VISITATION.

Carriers of His glory and love ignited a tremendous revival.

Prayer: *"Lord I also want a radical visitation and encounter with You. Please release the fiery whirlwind of Your Presence with fresh anointing and impartation of Your heart into my heart. I want an open heaven over my life. I want to hear what You hear and feel what You feel and know Your heart—My Beloved Bridegroom King—Jesus."*

Passion For Him,

Jill Austin
Psalm 91
(*"He who dwells in the secret place
 of the Most High
Shall abide under the shadow of
 The Almighty…."*)

JILL AUSTIN

"My greatest cry is a hunger for God."

We hear of conversions of sports figures, movie stars, drug and alcohol addicts, famous and infamous people, but one of the most unusual conversions is that of Master Potter Jill Austin, recognized artist, designer, and maker of pottery, prophet and preacher!

King James, Henry Higgins, Noah Webster, or Robert Funk, would scramble from their sarcophagus or tumble from their tomb to hear someone greet God with, "Hi God, What's up?" But we live in a **new generation, with new music, new voices, and a promise that great revival is and will come through the youth of our generation.** Jill Austin speaks intimately with God and appeals to and trains the younger generation. **For our generation,** she is known for her unique friendship with Holy Spirit and her ability to "impart radical hunger and passion for the Lord Jesus Christ." She also ministers to pastors, to saints and sinners, and imparts a hunger to the older generation **to intimately know and love God.**

Vibrant, enthusiastic, cheerleader at times, fiery passion for Jesus, charming with a sense of humor, quiet (at times) and compassionate, Jill Austin "treads where angels fear to tread,"--but always with a child-like spirit, and a powerful prophetic voice **for our generation.** God uses her prophetic gifting at times to shock people, but He gets their attention with the sole purpose of leading them to His Son.

When Jill sits in an airplane, in a business office, or at church, she *"starts looking for God. I can look at someone and ask Jesus what is happening in his or her life. It makes it a lot of fun. How can I pray?"* She calls this *"reading mail!"* God reveals things about the person that enables her to pray; she, in turn, may tell the person how God has spoken to her about his/her need. Of course the person may ask if she is psychic, *"How do you know that? How do you do that?"* Jill reveals that she is a Christian minister and before long she often leads the person to Christ!

Jill Austin, whose parents were both medical doctors, grew up as one of four children in Los Angeles, California, where she attended the Hollywood Presbyterian Church. She *"knew the Lord at the age of four,"* and at a very young age *"felt called to be a missionary and go to the nations.*" However, in her late teens, she "left the Lord" and became involved in the "Hippie Movement" that swept California in the late 1960's. In 1969, while attending a university in Washington, she re-dedicated her life to the Lord. From the University of Puget Sound, Tacoma, Washington, she received her B.F.A. majoring in pottery and sculpture and, later, earned the Fifth Year Secondary Teaching Degree. In 1979, she received a Master's degree from the University of Washington in Seattle, Washington, and became a production potter. As an award-winning "Master Potter" she made her living, for a time, as a professional artist exhibiting her pieces in many art shows and gaining a reputation in the Pacific Northwest. But God had other plans for her!

Jill has a natural love for color, art, and design. She loves taking a piece of clay, putting it on the wheel, watching it grow as though it has life that seems to live and breathe. She loves the kiln and the fire! God used this natural love for the process of producing fine pottery for the ministry to which he was calling her.

"Pottery is still a passion of my heart," Jill says. *"I love the yieldedness of the clay as I sit at the wheel. I'm always aware that any abrupt movement of my hands could tear the vessel.*

"The pottery process parallels our prophetic journeys. Jesus is the divine Potter and we are the yielded clay. Each vessel is His handiwork, unique and loved by Him.

"Through our lives our sinful choices are manifested as cracks, chips and brokenness. When a vessel becomes too broken it is pronounced 'worthless' and is discarded. That's when Master Potter comes on the scene, rescues the pot and begins to remake it. He does not disqualify us because of our weakness and vulnerability. He whispers in our ear His great love and incredible destiny for us—transforming us from weak broken vessels into His victorious Bride."

Master Potter Ministry started over thirty years ago with a small performing arts group. When Jill was not occupied in her trade, she would visit churches, bring a potter's wheel to the meetings and depict the Master Potter creating His clay vessels while actors illustrated the lives of the clay vessels. Combining music, drama and art, she brought the gospel of Jesus Christ to the lost, as well as deep healing to the broken-hearted.

Coming out of the 'Hippie Movement" and from a family who expressed little emotion, Jill describes her first encounters with churches where people were encouraged to raise their hands in praise and where people lingered after a sermon to give hugs and talk. Her encounters are filled with pathos and humor—rather than hug a person, she ran out and hugged a tree one time—but God patiently worked with her and ministered to her deep hurts, and continued to keep her on His potter's wheel so she, in turn, could minister to others!

Before the first presentation made at her local church, the pastor asked for a copy of her script. Not having a script and never using a script, she panicked and hid in a closet. As she finally came out and nervously walked across the stage, she began to illustrate the way God shapes us on a potter's wheel. She simply would say the words God spoke to her. At the end, people gave her a standing ovation and her ministry began to thrive. **Years later Jill discovered that her prophetic ministry began when God talked to her as she shaped the pottery on the wheel and she repeated to the audience what God said!** Sometimes she said she did not want to say or do the things God required, but when God said, *"Do you love Me enough to do it?"* she learned to obey. This time of grooming prepared her for the prophetic anointing and worldwide ministry and teaching she later would have.

From being a very frightened young person, a withdrawn, shy person, just coming out of the "Hippie Movement," Jill Austin obeyed God, and God later honored her in 2006 as one of many speakers at the One Hundredth Azusa Street Anniversary in Los Angeles, California! Austin's childlike faith, tenacity, commitment to stand for the purposes of God, and her **willingness to spend hours in prayer** have changed her into a much sought after conference speaker, ministering throughout the United States and in nations around the world. She literally has bridged international, denominational, and generational divides while on hundreds of ministry trips into Israel, New Zealand, Australia, Europe, Africa, Asia, and North America. Her vision is to see "historic revival where cities, nations, and entire continents are transformed by God's glory."

After Holy Spirit used Jill Austin in 1992 to help bring revival to New Zealand, Pastor Ian and Jan McCormack wrote, *"...the Lord* has mightily used her to bring revival into our personal life, the church, and the nation of New Zealand. She has also been used in starting a mighty move of the Holy Spirit in Australia. We personally recognize her as a woman of God, who, like Elijah, calls down fire from heaven—healing broken hearts, bringing fresh passion for Jesus and tangible power encounters with the anointing and Presence of God."

In 1983, Jill's Master Potter Ministries, located in Laguna Hills, California, was incorporated as a non-profit religious organization with its own governing Board of Directors. Jill has completed other certificates for Licensing and is an Ordained Minister. As Jill's ministry enlarged, testimonies abound over the years as to the accuracy of the governmental words released to churches, cities, and nations. At the beginning of the Gulf War, Jill sought God regarding the situation and God revealed to her that the war would last three days, which it did.

Jill has appeared on television programs such as the 700 Club, Praise the Lord, and TBN, as well as numerous radio talk shows. Her articles have been published in *Last Days Magazine*, *Spirit-Led Woman*, Enhance magazine, *Fresh Fire's Prophetic Destiny Journal*, *Kairos* magazine, *Ministries Today, Awe* magazine, Elijah List, and the *Women of Destiny Bible*.

To understand fully Jill's heart and message, a person needs to listen to her teachings available on cassette or CD, such as *Keys to the Anointing; Hearing the Voice of God; The Price Behind The Anointing;* and *Desperation, Visitation and Anointing.* Listening to the audio teaching, one becomes aware of the way God's Spirit is moving in a fresh way **in our generation** throughout the world. Every potential leader needs to hear *The Price Behind The Anointing.*

Austin is also a master storyteller and the author of two prophetic allegories, *Master Potter* and *Master Potter and The Mountain of Fire.* Using the biblical image describing the relationship of God and humanity as that of the potter and the clay, Jill's two books follow the story of a young woman named Forsaken, (portrayed at first as a broken clay pitcher) whose name is changed by the Master Potter to Beloved. The stories could be about anyone of us. *"God created us as earthenware vessels so we would realize our weakness and call out to Him. Each of our journeys takes us through much joy* and pain—but no person or situation is beyond hope; ...no one is too broken to be healed and used by God. There is no situation He can't redeem, for He is the God of second and third chances and he loves all His vessels."

Jill says God gave her a mandate to write the books "in order to pull back the curtains of the supernatural realm and **use these stories as something of a textbook on the Holy Spirit.**" The novels "unravel the mysteries of the glory realm, training you in spiritual warfare, hearing God's voice in every day life, and prayer intermingled with a love for the Word. ...**If the church begins to move in the power of the gospel, the world will not flock to the occult.**"

Having biblical foundations, the allegories "counter the current fascination with counterfeit spirituality—witchcraft, sorcery, New Age, Occultism, and demons. I hope," emphasizes Jill, "that these novels re-direct the Harry Potter generation into the loving arms of the Master Potter Himself. It's time someone warns that the demonic is dangerous to dabble with." The books are for all ages. Dr. Kingsley Fletcher said the "point most evident in Jill's writings is that God had made the choice to be ALL things to us. His delight is to usher us through life from beginning to end, concerning Himself with the small and big issues we face"....and that thought **is** mind-boggling!

Jill **dedicated** *Master Potter* **to the memory of her mother**, Elizabeth Isabelle Austin, a pioneer and forerunner, the only graduating female medical doctor in her class at the University of California, Berkley. She practiced medicine for 46 years. Jill lovingly said, "I know at first you didn't understand why I stopped being a professional potter and 'wasted' my teaching degree by going into full-time ministry and traveling with a rag-tag, struggling Christian performing arts group. But you stood in my corner and encouraged me to run for my dreams, and even made up the financial differences when love offerings were low or nonexistent.

"I'm glad you came to know Master Potter like I do and that you laughed your way into glory as you departed this world. You stand today with the great cloud of witnesses—still my cheerleader!"

Master Potter and The Mountain of Fire **is dedicated to her Best Friend Holy Spirit with this magnificent declaration:**

"How do I say thank you to my very best friend, Holy Spirit? What do I love the most about Him? Amazing grace—that's what He gives me. That's how He loves me and how He empowers me. His tender companionship and guidance always point to the glorious Son, Master Potter. Oh, how I love His violent love and insatiable fervency to bring suffering humanity to Jesus. I'm in awe that I can partner with Him to bring in the Harvest.

"High adventures! Walking with Him daily is never boring! He is not afraid of controversy or exposing religious doctrines and traditions of men. He is dangerous; He is not a tame God. We can't control or manipulate Him. At times He's like the roaring wind or consuming fire, but at other times He's like the gentle dove.

"Our relationship certainly hasn't been meek and mild. Often He is the one who gets me in trouble. Over the last 25 years of meetings I've been more or less the straight guy while Holy Spirit is a wild, heavenly tornado that wreaks havoc, shaking everything that can be shaken. Fear of man? He never has to deal with it; only I do, after He's offended many. But talking and wrestling late into the night I always see His great love and wisdom in challenging people to run for their highest callings.

"He fills the lonely places of my soul as His wind blows this traveling vagabond across this terrestrial globe. Always together, He's my confidant, counselor, and strategist. I love how He partners with me in ministry. It's as though He's standing right next to me whispering prophetic words and revelations, which proclaim destiny and birthright to many. He shows me insight into the Word and glimpses into eternity. He makes me homesick to be with Him forever.

"This wondrous Person, who is God, is so awesome and yet such an intimate friend. His colorful personality captivates my heart. My comprehension of Him has deepened over the years—never stagnant, forever growing. Amazing grace, that's what He gives me."

Jill Austin's vision is to train and equip people to move in the power of the Holy Spirit, not only in the church, but also in the secular marketplace with a demonstration of signs and wonders following. Jill says, "***Most of us in the Body of Jesus Christ have lost our desperation*** *for God. We want other people to go into the heavens and bring us back a three or four minute prophetic word. But we aren't willing to sacrifice to have the desperate hunger, to be willing to climb Mt. Sinai (as Moses did) ourselves! We have lost that passion and that desperate heart that says, God, we want to see lost souls won into the Kingdom! Lord, we want to be willing to risk our reputations and pray for the sick and for the brokenhearted. We want to pray for people not only at our church altars, but also on the streets, at our jobs, in our homes and wherever we feel Your prompting, God. Dear Jesus, **teach us**!"*

Listening to Jill, our generation <u>can learn</u> much about how to pray:

"*Oh, God, I am hungry, please talk to me! God, I have to know you. Lord, may we know You face to face? Give us Your heart for this decade, the decade of the harvest.*

"*Oh God, talk to me! God, I have to know You! I need to know You. I need to hear Your voice. Lord, wake me up in the middle of the night. Talk to me. Give me dreams and visions. Lord, I don't want to live my whole life in this place of apathy and living as though I am in a fog. Lord, I want clear vision and revelation. I want to be able to understand Your heart and to intimately know You. Lord, will you talk to me?*"

Jill says, "*I am in a real vulnerable place with Jesus, but I don't want it any other way! I have made a choice because I love Him! I have tried it all the other ways! You will die by being bored, by being lukewarm, by being restless, and knowing that you are missing your calling and your destiny.*"

"*When you come home do you say, 'Lord, here am I.' Or are you in a place where the only time you do Bible Study is for a few minutes and then have a few moments of prayer? Or do you stand up and start walking and praying, 'Oh God! God if there is anything in me, take it out. Oh, Jesus, I repent. Oh Lord, work on this and this, etc'."*

"God, here am I. Jesus, try the reins of my heart. Lord, show me what You want to do in me. Lord, show me where I am not trusting You and where I get afraid. Show me where I look at circumstances instead of keeping my eyes up to You.

*"It is very humbling! Then after He cleans me up, then **the next step is that I pray, 'Lord, can I minister to You? Lord, is there anything on Your heart?** Lord, You have this great big world and I want to be Your friend. Lord, I know Your heart aches. There are so many who are lost. There are so many that have left You, have been offended by You because they haven't gotten their way when they wanted it. Like spoiled kids, they have left You, Lord.*

"So I go before God and ask Him what is on His heart. Many times I will just weep and cry because I feel His heart and I love Him. He isn't just an 'it'; He isn't just a power. He is God! He is wonderful! I want relationship."

In treating Holy Spirit as an intimate friend, Jill encourages us to ask questions. During her public meetings, she partners with Holy Spirit and follows Him as He leads her. She is not afraid to ask God questions: How do You want me to pray? How do You want us to begin? She encourages the audience to ask God questions.

Jill speaks to all ages. She challenges the "retired" generation with her declaration,, *"I tell you, there is no such thing as retirement! It's not retirement—it's reFIREment! We try to retire when we are old. John was old, yet he was given the most prophetic revelation in the New Testament to show us the end-time church. God is not retiring you and there is no mid-life crisis. If you are buying into it, then you are buying into the world's thinking. You are not buying into the Gospel, into the Word of God. Most of the men who were used so powerfully in the Word of God were in the fall and the winter of their lives. God met Moses at eighty years of age, when he felt he couldn't even talk and that there was no purpose to his life."*

She stimulates and dares the Joshua Generation—God's Younger Generation—to go beyond the four walls of the church and move in radical exploits for God. *"The Holy Spirit is working in this hour to bring forth the new revolutionists who move with fire and unction in*

His Spirit. The Lord is bringing forth a new generation—one that will yield to the leading of the Holy Spirit to rise up against evil in these last days. I want to pass on my baton to this next generation...a baton that is dripping with oil and not some dried up old stick!"

Jill urges all of us that just as in the Bible the Priests used to go daily into the Temple to trim wicks and pour in fresh oil, we have to go to the Throne to Jesus (*"You can't have my oil!"*) and get our own oil! Each one of us individually has a journey of going to the Throne and crying out and saying, *"Oh God! Give us fresh oil. Lord, where the oil is old, take out the old and put in the new!"*

Jill's prayer for each of her messages and books is that "revelation and impartation" be released. And we **do** come away with a hunger for a demonstration of the Holy Spirit, a cry to know God more intimately, a cry for God to talk to us in dreams and visitations!

"Arise, and go down to the potter's house,
and there I will cause you to hear My words.
Then I went down to the potter's house,
and there he was, making something at the wheel.
And the vessel that He made of clay was
marred in the hand of the potter,
so He made it again into another vessel,
as it seemed good to the potter to make.
Then the word of the Lord came to me,
saying: . . .
'can I not do with you as this potter'?
says the Lord.
'Look, as the clay is in the potter's hand,
so are you in My hand'. . . ."

--Jeremiah 18:2-6

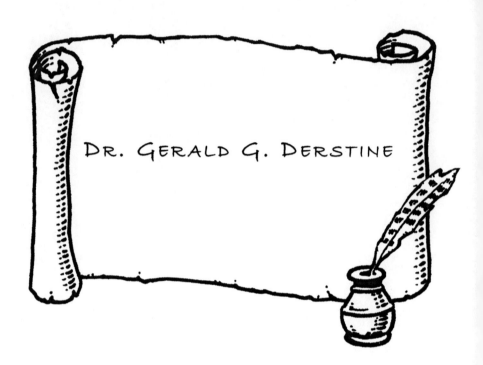

DR. GERALD G. DERSTINE

CHRISTIAN RETREAT
STRAWBERRY LAKE

Gerald Derstine
Founder, President

33991 Victory Way Dr.
Ogema, MN 56569

Reservations and
Business Office
218/983-3217
1-888-593-2882
FAX
218/983-4071

WEB SITE
www.Strawberrylake.org

Apr.l 12, 2004

To Whom This may Concern:

The first seven days of 1955 totally changed my family lifestyle. God Answered our prayers for Revival. My book entitled "Following the FiRe" detAils the Account. This move of God continues to impAct Mennonite communities and Nations Around the world.

Today as of this writing we have
CHRISTIAN RETREAT, BradentoN, Florida
CHRISTIAN RETREAT Family Church, BRADENTON, Fl.
STRAWbery LAKE CHRISTIAN RETREAT CHURCH, Inc. Ogema Minn.
North Country CHRISTIAN RETREAT, HERMAN, N.Y.
A.C.T. TRuck Ministries, RoAD Angel TRuckStop, BroomsTown, ILLinois
ISRAEL AFFAIRS INTERNATIONAL, BRADentoN, FLorida
Gospel CRusADe Ministerial Fellowship
Gospel CRusADe, Inc. (Founding organization of All Above ministries)

More than 3000 churches in 48 Nations of the world Are under the covering of this ministry, since 1955.

Strawberry Lake Christian Retreat Church, Inc.
Affiliated with Gospel Crusade, Inc. : Bradenton, Florida

Gerald Derstine

1200 Glory Way Blvd.
BRADENTON, Fl. 34212

GERALD DERSTINE

April 12, 2004

To Whom This May Concern:

The first seven days of 1955 totally changed my family lifestyle. God answered our prayers for revival. My book entitled "Following The Fire" details the account. This move of God continues to impact Mennonite communities and nations around the world.

Today as of this writing we have
Christian Retreat, Bradenton, Florida
Christian Retreat Family Church, Bradenton, Fl.
Strawberry Lake Christian Retreat Church, Inc., Ogema, Minn.
North Country Christian Retreat, Herman, N.Y.
A.C.T. Truck Ministries, Road Angel Truckstop, Brownstown, Illinois
Israel Affairs International, Bradenton, Florida
Gospel Crusade Ministerial Fellowship
Gospel Crusade, Inc. (Founding organization of all above ministries)

More than 3000 churches in 48 nations of the world are under the covering of this ministry, since 1955.

Gerald Derstine

Dr. Gerald G. Derstine

"A mediator for Jesus Christ"

So unusual was the "divine visitation" Dr Gerald Derstine experienced on an Indian reservation in Minnesota in the 1950's, his testimony is included with sixty other <u>Voices of</u> <u>Pentecost</u> in Dr. Vinson Synan's book by the same name--testimonies of lives "touched by the Holy Spirit." Besides a portion of Derstine's story, the book includes such famous people as St. Augustine, Oswald Chambers, Charles Finney, St. Francis of Assisi, and Dwight L. Moody. To our generation, Dr. Derstine has been a mediator between God and His people for many souls around the world.

Of German descent, Gerald G. Derstine was born in Eastern Pennsylvania and reared in a strict conservative Mennonite home. As a young person, to compensate for his small size and his speech impediment of stuttering, he excelled in basketball and anything having to do with music--playing the accordion, piano, or organ (none of which was permitted in his Mennonite church). *"My stuttering was an embarrassing handicap, yet I refused to let it control my life. I determined that even if I would always be a stammerer, I would still make something of myself."* It was this natural determination that God used throughout Gerald's life.

As a boy of nine when he heard his Uncle Llewelyn Groff, a missionary to the Chippewa Indians tell about his adventures, Gerald Derstine said his heart started to beat faster. *"I heard no voices, but I knew, I just knew that one day I would be a missionary. Beyond a shadow of doubt I knew."* But it wasn't until after he was married that he gave his life to Jesus Christ.

When he met and fell in love with Beulah Hackman, (the girl who at 16 had her own car and a heavy foot on the pedal!) neither of them was a Christian, but when he proposed to Beulah he blurted out, *"W-would you still want to m-marry me if I were to be a preacher or m-minister someday? I mean, w-would you b-be willing to s-spend your life as a p-preacher's wife?"* Beulah accepted his proposal!

Looking back, he remembers being troubled by a disturbing reoccurring dream. *"In that dream I was preaching—not only to a* congregation of white, American faces, but to black and Oriental faces. It was nonsensical for me to have dreams like that, especially since I knew I wasn't even living a Christian life."

After they were married Derstine and his wife heard about "faith healers," T.L. Osborn and Gordon Lindsay, holding meetings in a tent revival. Out of curiosity they attended and from this influence accepted Jesus Christ. Derstine became interested in reading the Bible and read it so much that his mother warned him that it just was not normal. *"You shouldn't get so serious about it. I mean you could lose your mind if you keep up what you're doing. I don't want you ending up in some mental institution."*

Having heard also of the healing power of Jesus Christ, soon Derstine was searching the Word for verses about healing. Within six weeks, from diligently applying the Word, he discovered one morning that his speech was normal; he no longer stuttered!

Gerald Derstine and his wife began handing out gospel tracts, at least 1,000 tracts every weekend in Philadelphia's downtown "bawdy Market Street." About his education Derstine said, *"Those inebriated winos were my Bible school teachers. Those dirty ghetto streets were my seminary hallways, and the cost of the tracts, hamburgers, and coffee was my tuition. They were the only people in a big city I had nerve enough to speak to."*

Within a short time his Uncle Llewelyn invited him to come help in the mission work on the reservation. Derstine and his wife moved to the reservation and Gerald said, *"Amid the hardship, I had that deep-down calm of knowing we were in the Lord's will. There was a great sense of fulfillment in helping these poverty-stricken people and for the first time I felt a real purpose in life."*

Later, he was asked to become the pastor of the Strawberry Lake Mennonite Church. *"I had a burden for these people, most of whom had joined the church through my contact with them over a cup of coffee and Watkins salves* (a way to supplement his income) *laid out on the table."* It was here that he and his assistant pastor decided to pray earnestly for revival. For a year they met from 5:30 to 6:30 a.m. and fasted on Wednesday and Friday till three in the afternoon, "the ninth hour." He had read somewhere that *"the early Christians did this."* They also asked the congregation to join them in prayer for revival among the Mennonite community.

In December 1954, God began to answer their prayers, suddenly, and beyond what they had asked for!

The story told in **Following The Fire** of the outpouring of the Holy Spirit in the Mennonite community is a story **our generation and future generations** need to hear. In answer to the yearlong prayers, a most unusual revival began when seventy-three young people attended a (holiday) five-day vacation Bible school at the Loman Mennonite Church, 200 miles from Derstine's church. As an "outing" all seventy-three young people volunteered to go to International Falls for a street meeting. They sang on the street corner and then, to get out of the cold, were invited inside by a department store manager. They were given permission to sing carols. Suddenly, a girl who had just been saved a day earlier tapped Rev. Derstine on the shoulder asking him if she could give her testimony (something unheard of in this Mennonite group); others started volunteering to give their testimony to people who began gathering in the store. Rev. Derstine became uneasy! Back at the school that night, instead of classes being conducted, testimonies went on—all seventy-three wanted to testify. Then some of the students began weeping (**again an improper thing to do**) over lost parents. From that point on for a whole week, a visitation of the Holy Spirit occurred such as many in **our generation have never witnessed**.

God does have a sense of humor! At one point Derstine's **staid** Mennonite uncle who was also the school's principal, tried to "drag a student to the cloakroom." When Derstine asked him what he was doing, Uncle Llewelyn said, *"Well, I think he might be speaking in tongues and if he is I understand someone has to give an interpretation **or else they're out of order**. So we have to get them out of the sanctuary at least."*

Rev. Derstine tried to keep his composure and figure out what was going on. There was a clatter, a thump, and young people were falling off their chairs onto the floor and shaking. Derstine wondered what had happened after such a lovely day. *"Has the devil gotten in?"* Derstine thought, *"I wish there weren't so many guests here tonight. What will they think?"* After consulting with some of the teachers they decided to sing "There Is Power in the Blood." Things got worse. Somewhere he had read about being able to "plead the blood of Jesus" if an evil spirit overtook a person. *"We circled around each person on the floor, put our hands on them and began repeating, 'I plead the blood of Jesus'."* As soon as they did that, the shaking and trembling not only didn't stop, it got worse!

The young people saw visions of heaven, some saw Jesus, and some lay in "trances" prophesying about world events that would occur. (**Derstine reminded God that all he had prayed for was a revival for his community. He wanted to see souls saved and that was all!**) *"As each young person ended his message he would invariably say, 'this is my body you see, this is my voice you hear, but this is from the Lord.' One word at a time."*

One recently saved boy instructed the group to turn to Acts 2:17 and 18 *"and you shall understand."* (Derstine did not understand!) Derstine began reading to the group: *"And it shall come to pass in the last days, saith God, I will pour out of my Spirit upon all flesh; and your sons and your daughters shall prophesy, and your young men shall see visions, and your old men shall dream dreams: And on my servants and on my handmaidens I will poor out in those days of my Spirit; and they shall prophesy."*

One prophecy came forth from an Amish boy: *"The sword of the Spirit is the Word of the Lord! There shall be revival taking place on this earth like man has never witnessed in the history of the world— even greater than what took place on the day of Pentecost!"* The prophecy went on: *"No man nor any organization will receive any of the glory in this revival, but only the Lord thy God! He could have used a mule or an animal to bring this revival, but since he made man in His own likeness and image, He shall use man! This revival has thus far gone only as far as one and one-half drops in a ten-quart pail in comparison to what shall take place on this earth."*

However, there was much opposition. As God revealed Himself to the young people, to the same degree the devil revealed himself. One neighbor at 5:30 a.m. came to Derstine's house yelling, *"I have come to settle this thing right now!"* Derstine was surprised to see how angry a previously friendly neighbor could be. He was boiling mad; his face flushed and contorted into a snarl by anger. *"I'm sick and tired of all this religious nonsense!"* he continued to yell. *"I came here tonight to beat you all up—all of you! I want all the people in this house to come outside so I can beat 'em up. Right now!"*

Suddenly, the man turned and went home (after the group told him how much they cared about him and that God loved him)!

Most of the young people became "shunned" after the weeklong experience. When Amos (born in the Amish faith) went home after the visitation, he was not allowed to eat at the same table with his family.

A prophesy given by one of the young people to Rev. Derstine was, "*Gerald, you are to be separated from the Mennonite church, but do not fear, for* **I shall give you a greater ministry.** *I will take you to the outer edges of the Mennonite communities. You shall minister to and teach many people about the things of my Spirit. I am going to take you into the cities. From city to city you shall go, ministering unto multitudes and thousands of my people, teaching them the things of my Spirit."* **Much to Derstine's dismay, in a few weeks time the Bishops visited him asking him to renounce the events that had occurred. They told him it was necessary that he be temporarily silenced from ministering in the Mennonite church**. "*Gerald, I know you believe what you have gone through was of God,* **but it's just not the Mennonite way.** *We're going to have to silence you from the Mennonite church and ask you not to minister any longer..."*

Dr. Derstine moved his family to Florida, and, for some time, became a tent revival preacher establishing churches as he ministered. But God had not forgotten Derstine, his broken heart, and his cry for revival among his Mennonite people. After being invited to share his testimony at the International Convention of the Full Gospel Business Men's Fellowship in Los Angeles, his life was drastically changed. Churches of all denominations invited him to give his testimony. Doors opened for him to tell of the mighty visitation. (*"From city to city you shall go, and you shall minister to multitudes...teaching them about the things of my Spirit."*) The earlier prophecy was coming to pass, but always **Derstine's question to God was "*What about our people, the Mennonites?*" Again he was reminded, "*They shall not understand now, but they shall later.*"**

Derstine believed the people whose lives had been touched by the phenomenal revival "*needed to have an opportunity to really understand what had happened.*" Years later the thought struck him, "*Why not start a Christian camp, a place where Christian families would go in the summer and relax; at the same time, they would be taught about the things of God."* Ten years after God had visited them with revival, he felt led to return to Strawberry Lake to set up a summer Christian retreat facility, one-quarter mile from the little Mennonite church he had pastored.

Later, they were given the opportunity to develop a "similar place of retreat" in Bradenton, Florida, a *"one-of-its-kind, year-round conference center where retirees, young people and families live, and where thousands of people come to be strengthened in the faith."*

Restoration does come. In 1975, in Landisville, Pennsylvania, at a Mennonite Renewal Conference, Derstine was informally welcomed back into the church. The prophecy given twenty years earlier was finally being fulfilled as Gerald was asked to speak at his alma mater, Eastern Mennonite College, "on the things of the Holy Spirit." In 1977, he was invited to a Holy Spirit Conference conducted by the Mennonite church near Goshen, Indiana, where he was *"accepted in the brotherhood and told to continue in my present ministry."* In June 1998, Dr. Derstine and his wife were invited back to Strawberry Lake Mennonite Church where "the phenomenal outpouring of the Holy Spirit" swept through the sanctuary the last week of 1954. He had been invited to speak on the church's 50th anniversary celebration. (There he saw many of the young people, now parents and grandparents, who had been a part of the unusual revival forty years before.)

Dr. Derstine, the author of twelve books, is president of Christian Retreat and Gospel Crusade, Inc., and with his wife Beulah and their four children—Joanne, Philip, Timothy, Stephen—they are all involved in carrying on the ministry. His dream to teach Truth on the subject of the Holy Spirit and Kingdom of God principles and to "bring a prophetic message to the churches regarding the time in which we live" is being fulfilled. The "camp facilities" are known for their many creative **outreaches** and "unconventional soul winning."

Not only for the Mennonite people but also for the Jewish people, Dr. Derstine has been burdened. Fifty times he has been in Israel, and the Israeli government has honored him. In 1987, the secretary of the Prime Minister of Israel invited him to come to Israel. At that meeting he was asked to be a **peace mediator** between Jews and Arabs!

On the 100-acre campus in Bradenton, Florida, at Christian Retreat one experiences a **spiritual unity**—unity in worship, in fellowship, in purpose. *"Here one finds Catholics, Episcopalians, Lutherans, Methodists, Presbyterians, Pentecostals, Mennonites and others uniting in praise and worship of their Savior and Lord and seeking to serve Him."*

Dr. Gerald Derstine, **a mediator for our generation**, now asks, *"Why should I be so amazed that God had chosen the northern Minnesota woods, on an Indian reservation, in the middle of winter, to start His fire burning in the Mennonite church"?*

"For I will pour water on
him who is thirsty,
and floods on the dry ground;
I will pour My Spirit
on your descendants,
and My blessing on your offspring;..."
--Isaiah 44:3

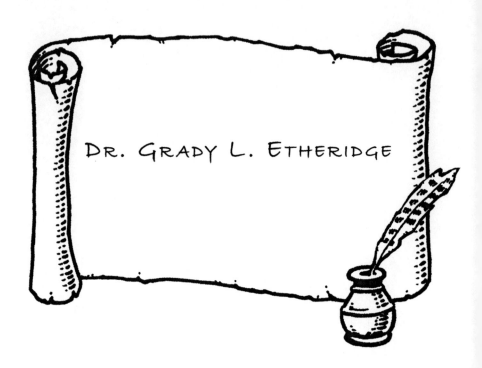

DR. GRADY L. ETHERIDGE

G&M ETHERIDGE
MINISTRIES, INC.
Ministry of Freedom and Joy

Ph. 573-471-9244
Orders: 573-763-3679

Gandy L. Etheridge
July 26, 1923 - Jan 14, 2004

As a minister I have belonged to the Southern Baptist Convention from age 8 to (1969) 56 I retired to become an independent evangelist. 1986

In 1973 the Foreign Mission Board of the Southern Baptist Convention asked me to go to Africa to conduct some city-wide evangelistic crusades. Five of leaders and evangelists went to Nigeria.

After one crusade was finished we traveled by car from southern to northern Nigeria a trip of about 450 miles. The temperature was 120°. We became thirsty and decided to stop for a Coke.

The place where we stopped was a short distance from the service station where the Cokes were being. When I found out the Cokes were not refrigerated I volunteered to stay with the Van and watch over the luggage while the others went for the drinks.

Out of the "bush" came about 100-200 men begging holding out little pans. I refused to give them anything because there were too many. Things got so confusing I really couldn't tell for sure how many there were. I said "no, no, get away." They began to press in as if they were going to rob me. The Holy Spirit rose up inside me and I began preaching to them in a language I did not know

P.O. Box 564, Sikeston, MO 63801-0564
www.gmstministries.org   myrna@onemain.com

they began to back away — then run. The missionaries with the cokes and asked me what happened, I really didn't know for sure, so I told them, I just told them to get away, and they began to run. None of these Baptist men believed in speaking in tongues so I didn't tell them that part of the story.

When the Nigerian men ran they went to a near-by school where a pastor from that area was teaching comparative religions in a muslim school. These men asked him how to be "born-again". They told him that a man preached to them along side the road in their language about salvation in Jesus Christ.

The result was very outstanding. The pastor opened his church for evangelistic services and in a week over 1500 men had been converted to Christianity not counting the women and children which would have been over 3000 total.

That pastor Rev. Gabriel Ajadi rode his motor-bike 90 miles to ask us to come and help him. We were conducting a revival crusade in a football stadium. He told us that after I preached in their (Hausa) language along side the road revival broke out in his little village many people were saved.

The end of the story is: I met Gabriel on an airplane 2 years later coming to America to enter college. I helped him go all the way through until he received his doctrate. He returned home to Nigeria to become a teacher in a seminary in Ogbomosho, Nigeria where he resides today with his family of six.

Grady L. Etheridge

GRADY L. ETHERIDGE

As a minister I have belonged to the Southern Baptist Convention from age 8 to (1969) 56. I retired to become an independent evangelist. (1986)

In 1973 The Foreign Mission Board of the Southern Baptist Convention asked me to go to Africa to conduct some city-wide evangelistic crusades. Five of leaders and evangelists went to Nigeria.

After one crusade was finished we traveled by car from southern to northern Nigeria a trip of about 450 miles. The temperature was 120 degrees. We became thirsty and decided to stop for a Coke.

The place where we stopped was a short distance from the service station where the Cokes were located. When I found out the Cores were not refrigerated I volunteered to stay with the van and watch over the luggage while the others went for the drinks.

Out of the "bush" came about 100-200 men begging, holding out little pans. I refused to give them anything because there were too many. Things got so confusing I really couldn't tell for sure how many there were. I said, "No, no, get away." They began to press in as if they were going to rob me. The Holy Spirit rose up inside me and I began preaching to them in a language I did not know. They began to back away—then run. The missionaries with the Cokes [came] and asked me what happened. I really didn't know for sure, so I told them, I just told them to get away and they began to run. None of these Baptist men believed in speaking in tongues so I didn't tell them that part of the story.

When the Nigerian men ran they went to a near-by school where a pastor from that area was teaching comparative religions in a Muslim school. These men asked him how to be "born-again." They told him that a man preached to them along side the road in their language about salvation in Jesus Christ.

The result was very outstanding. The pastor opened his church for evangelistic services and in a week over 1500 men had been converted to Christianity, not counting the women and children which would have been over 3000 total.

That pastor, Rev. Gabriel Ajodi, rode his motorbike 90 miles to ask us to come and help him. We were conducting a revival crusade in a football stadium. He told us that after I preached in their (Hausa) language along side the road revival broke out in his little village. Many people were saved.

The end of the story is: I met Gabriel on an airplane 2 years later coming to America to enter college. I helped him go all the way through until he received his doctorate. He returned home to Nigeria to become a teacher in a seminary in Ogbomosho, Nigeria, where he resides today with his family of six.

Grady L. Etheridge

Dr. Grady L. Etheridge

"The Pastor's Pastor"

Zacchaeus first met God in a sycamore tree (Luke 19:4); David met God in the sheep pasture (1 Samuel 16:11); the apostle Paul met God on the back of a horse--or on the ground after he was knocked off (Acts 9:4); the paralytic met God as he was let down through the roof (Mark 2:10); and the powerful Ethiopian met Christ in his chariot (Acts 8:26-37).

Dr. Grady L. Etheridge met Jesus Christ in a "pea patch," as his mother, working in the garden, stopped what she was doing and prayed with her eight-year-old son! **Our generation honors Dr. Etheridge** for sixty-six years of serving God and fulfilling the Great Commission throughout the world.

At sixteen years of age, as Grady was building a fire for a stove in the church, he had another unusual spiritual encounter when he heard God speak saying he would become a minister. He ran to the pastor's home, told him, and then to his home, and told his mother who "floured the kitchen" as she praised the Lord!

Dr. Etheridge prepared himself. He attended Baylor University and Biola College in Los Angeles. He has two degrees in Bible theology, the Ph.B.D and Graduate Theology from Pioneer College in Illinois, and an M.T. (Masters in Theology) from International College of Bible Theology, Illinois. In addition, he has been granted two Doctor of Divinity degrees. One is from International College of Bible Theology and the other from United Full Gospel Ministers and Churches, Inc. of California.

Since he believes radio and television to be the greatest vehicle for getting the gospel out, he has been interested especially in communications. His outreach has included diversified work with Channel 27 at Marion, Illinois. He and his wife, Myrna, have been frequent guests on "Joy" with Jim McClellan and Friday "Praise the Lord" programs at various Trinity Broadcasting Networks in California, Indiana, New York, and Colorado. He has taught on www.TCT.TV and "School of the Bible" programs worldwide.

From a sod house in West Texas, he has gone to the world preaching the gospel. Many know of Total Christian Television

Network (www.tct.tv) and School of the Bible program that airs weekly using eighteen stations in the U.S.A. and covers 170 nations of the world through ten satellites. He served for a time in pioneer missions where he was instrumental in helping start and structure **eighteen new churches** and missions and **two accredited colleges**. His evangelistic outreach has included Russia, Eastern Europe, Nigeria, Ghana, and the Dominican Republic. At one time he was an official guest with Astronaut James Irwin and Nora Lam in the People's Republic of China at Peking.

Dr. Etheridge is an encourager and will sometimes schedule a series of meetings to encourage the pastor. The Holy Spirit makes Dr. Etheridge's ministry draw people to the love of Jesus. Many call him the Pastor's Pastor. One pastor said, *"You make me feel so good about the ministry and all the difficult things get back into proportion. You encourage all of us to remain faithful."* He and his wife sometimes minister together, and "miracles happen in every service." As God instructs him to do, Dr. Etheridge carries a special anointing to bless a person in the handling of finances, More than evangelism, the great commission includes the command to disciple people, *"teaching them all I have taught you"* (Matthew 28:20)," and Dr. Grady Etheridge has fulfilled that command.

Dr. Etheridge and his wife live in Missouri, and he has one daughter, Karan Thatcher of Seattle, Washington. Friends know two closely guarded secrets: he is talented in drawing cartoons, and some evenings, he will request a trip to "get an ice cream cone." When he is asked about retirement, in a relaxed manner, as he's reading the Bible exploring the latest new thought about a scripture, he quips, "I didn't find that in the Bible and besides I don't have time for that!"

Oh, how great is Your goodness,
which You have laid up for those who
fear, revere, and worship You;
goodness which You have wrought for
those who trust and take refuge in You
before the sons of men!
In the secret of Your presence You
hide them from the plots of men;
You keep them secretly in Your
pavilion from the strife of tongues.
-- Psalm 31:19-20

"I Have Asked But This Of You"

"By nightfall the great rock upon which Moses had spoken was vacant, except for one lone figure. Unobserved by all, He had been there listening—listening to Moses recount to the people His very own message to them. Afterward He had walked among His people, listening intently to their every word.

"A deep sadness now disturbed the face of the Lord, for He was contemplating the response He had heard from His people.

"A long, deep groan of sorrow, unheard by human ears but shattering the tranquility of the entire heavenly host, rose up from His depths.

"'I did not require of you
your wealth nor coins of gold.
What need have I of these?
I did not ask of you that you serve Me.
Do I, the Mighty One,
Need to be waited upon?
Neither did I ask of you
Your worship nor your prayers
Nor even your obedience.'

"He paused. Once more a long, mournful groan rose from His breast.

**"'I have asked but this of you;
that you love Me…
love Me…
love Me.'"**

**--from Chapter 17, *THE DIVINE ROMANCE*,
Gene Edwards**

Handwriting

convinces

others

about

your

identity!

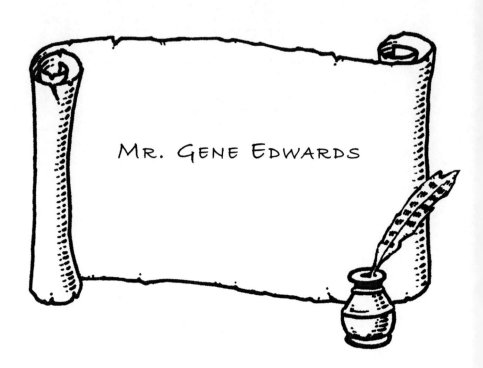

MR. GENE EDWARDS

At the Request of Verva-Lea Turner

It has always been my impression that all things which await us in the other senses can be touched or a foretaste. I also assumed there was one exception: that of being one with God — that is the utter lostness in God — which may be our final state.

There was a day, in 1964 (approximately) I — in realms of which I cannot discuss — I ceased to exist and was quite lost in God. A foretaste of union — oneness — and even dissolution in God.

Gene Edwards

Oct. 11-04

P.O. Box 3450 • Jacksonville, FL 32206 • (904) 598-2347 Fax: (904) 598-3456

GENE EDWARDS

It has always been my impression that all things which await us in other realms can be touched as a foretaste. I also assessed there was one exception: that of being one with God—that is the ultra lostness in God—which may be our final state.

There was a day, in 1964 (circa) that I—in realms of which I cannot describe—I ceased to exist and was quite lost in God. A foretaste of one-on-oneness and our dissolution in God.

Gene Edwards
Oct. 11-04

GENE EDWARDS

FROM "FORGETTABLE" TO "UNFORGETTABLE"
("God's voice thunders in marvelous ways; He does great things beyond our understanding."—Job 37:5)

No wonder the **Scripture** extols the great and marvelous things the Lord can do! Imagine a young boy dyslexic, color blind, incredibly shy, not able to spell, and "no one could read his handwriting." Imagine the same boy becoming America's foremost Christian storyteller with one of his books, <u>The Divine Romance</u>, listed as one of three most requested books in Christian stores!** The recorder chooses to believe God can do great and marvelous deeds (*"Praise be to the Lord God, the God of Israel, who alone does marvelous deeds."*--Psalm 72:18).

Most things about Gene Edwards' life **are** a paradox. How could he attend a seminary, pastor a church, be an evangelist, author some thirty books, plant churches throughout the world, and yet, grow up in a small town in Texas as the son of an oilfield worker, in a "tough, brawling world of oilfield roughnecks"? How could he have graduated from college at eighteen years of age with a B.S. in English literature, and in 1951, be the youngest college graduate ever to enroll at Southwestern Baptist Theological Seminary in Fort Worth, Texas? How could he have spent his first full year of theological training in Europe as the result of being the one American selected to be the student representing America at a Seminary in Zurich, Switzerland, **and yet**, in grammar school (sitting in the back of the class, never uttering a word, and hoping no one would ask him a question) be labeled with severe "learning problems," and as he said, be "very forgettable"? Nevertheless, Gene Edwards was or did all of the above!

** In a poll taken of bookstore managers they were asked What books written in the twentieth century do you think are timeless and will still be on bookstore shelves 100 years from now? Three books made that list: Oswald Chambers, <u>My Utmost for His Highest</u>; C.S. Lewis', <u>Mere Christianity</u>; and **Gene Edwards', <u>The Divine Romance</u>.**

Our generation will probably remember Gene Edwards for his unsurpassed, God-given imagination and anointing to tell a story. Retelling many of the powerful and beautiful stories based on Biblical incidents and characters, Edwards causes people to use their imagination, think, and draw closer to God. For example, in *The Prisoner In The Third Cell* Edwards looks into "what John the Baptist may have thought about being put in prison." Somewhat in the manner of C.S. Lewis, the book reveals "what John must have thought about Jesus being the Messiah." In *The Divine Romance,* the story of the Crucifixion and Resurrection is presented from the view of angels, and the entire book has been called "the greatest love story ever told". Some of his books have been turned into plays performed by professionals on stage and enacted in simple dramas in churches.

Edwards has a *"prodigious memory and a passion for history and literature,"* but after taking a writing course at Scarritt College in How to Write for Semi-Literates, he says he writes books *"on about a fourth grade level....the same level I do mathematics!"* Of those 34 plus books, most are done in a series containing two or more books within that given subject. For example, The Chronicles of Heaven include *Christ Before Creation* and *The Return*; *An Introduction to the Deeper Christian Life* includes *Living by the Highest Life, The Secret to the Christian Life, The Inward Journey;* Revolutionary Books on Church Life include *Revolution and How to Meet in Homes,* etc.; Books on comfort and inner healing include *A Tale of Three Kings, The Prisoner In the Third Cell,* etc; and The First-Century Diaries include *The Silas Diary. The Titus Diary,* etc.

When Gene was three years old, he contacted scarlet fever and for days was near death. Both parents prayed, *"Lord, if you let him live, we give him wholly and completely to You!"* He lived, and on the day before his **seventeenth**** birthday Gene was converted to Christ, which among other benefits, resulted in the beginning of his being torn "away from the moorings of shyness." That was the beginning of an exciting life filled with education, travel, ministry, and writing.

———————————
**I include the age because so many people mightily used of God, date their conversion to the age 17 (sometimes earlier)

When he was 17 and she was 19, Gene Edwards met Helen Rogers (who was planning to go to the mission field). At the age of twenty-one Gene married Helen in Studio B at Rockefeller Plaza in New York City on national television before 6,000,000 viewers! They were married by Dr. Frank Laubach on an NBC TV program called "Bride and Groom,"—a program that invited couples with interesting stories to tell their love story. (Dr. Laubach was the famous reading teacher who, at the invitation of governments, traveled worldwide to set up programs teaching people how to read and write.)

Then life began to change for Gene Edwards. For many years, even though he had written books and was training leaders in various denominations about personal evangelism, there was a "desperation going on inside" of him, "a sense that he worked from out of the soul, not the spirit." He said he had always been a "do-er" and not a "be-er." **He said he sensed** *"None of us knew Christ very well."*

One of the pivotal points leading to this decision was **a discourse** that took place in a seminary class attended by Edwards, other ministers, and seminary students:

> Seminary professor: *"What is the main thing, **the central issue**, for which we stand?"*
> One seminarian student: *"Baptism by immersion."*
> Professor: *"No, that is not correct."*
> Another student: *"The security of the believer."*
> Professor: *"No, that is not correct."*
> Another student: *"We stand for the Bible as being the infallible Word of God."*
> Again, a negative.
> The professor finally gave the answer: *"**The centrality of all that any church or Christian should stand for is Jesus Christ**."*

At the age of twenty-nine, believing he never belonged in the pastorate, Edwards cancelled speaking engagements, took the next year off to seek God, to do research, to write, and to **know Christ better**. He invited Christ to "**live His life out from me.**" No longer would he seek to serve God; *"whatever happens will be what You do. You will be the One living my life."* Edwards said, *"The real* *god to whom we bow down to is the god of serving God. I gave up that god, the god of serving Christ. **Now it is Christ.**"*

During this "searching" time he wove together what turned out to be the history of the 1st Christian Century. After a period of nearly 40 years he began publishing the five volume set telling the story of the First-Century Christians—their customs and conditions of the day, the nautical, political, meteorological, religious, and military world.

In the 1960's Edwards played a leading role in the "Jesus Movement." To minister to these college students gathered in 1969 in an auditorium at U.C.L.A. was one of the most important projects "having eternal value" that he had accomplished. Up to this time, Gene felt "nothing was worthy of being called a ministry." Known as the **U.C.L.A. Tape**, the audio tape of the message became the most listened to tape of "The Jesus Movement."

The last twenty-five years, Edwards has traveled the world helping to set up churches more like those of the First Century and producing books (He says he has five more he wants to do), such as *The Christian Woman...Set Free.* He teaches people how to know Christ better. His concern is "While I am speaking, do the words I speak and the message I bring indicate a present, up-to-date, experiential, daily, intimate encounter with my Lord?"

Though Gene Edwards has lived an interesting life, written many books, ministered in all parts of the world, and won many accolades, he has one desire. I believe he would most desire to be **remembered by our generation** as an author/speaker who has made Jesus Christ his Lord, that he daily has an encounter with his Lord, and that he desires to teach other people how to walk in that fellowship! He would desire to be remembered as one who taught us how to **love, love, love our Lord!**

"To fall in love with God is the greatest of all romances! To seek Him is the greatest of all achievements! To find Him is the greatest human achievement!"—Raphael Simon

The Lover To His Beloved:

"And therefore the Lord (earnestly) waits
(expectant, looking, and longing)
to be gracious to you,
and therefore He lifts Himself up
that He may have mercy on you
and show loving kindness to you;
for the Lord is a God of justice.
Blessed—happy, fortunate (to be envied) are
all who (earnestly) wait for Him,
who expect and look and long for Him
(for His victory, His favor, His love,
His peace, His joy, and His matchless,
unbroken companionship)."
--Isaiah 30:18 (Amp)

WHEN THE SPIRIT OF TRUTH COMES

"But when the Helper comes, whom I shall send to you from the Father, the Spirit of truth who proceeds from the Father, He will testify of Me."—John 15:26

"And it happened, while Apollos was at Corinth, that Paul, having passed through the upper regions, came to Ephesus. And finding some disciples he said to them, 'Did you receive the Holy Spirit when you believed?' So they said to him, 'We have not so much as heard whether there is a Holy Spirit'."

--Acts 2:38-39

"And when Paul had laid hands on them, the Holy Spirit came upon them, and they spoke with tongues and prophesied."
--Acts 19:6

MRS. JUANITA F. ESSERT

My most profound encounter with
our wonderful Lord was the night I
was baptized in His Holy Spirit, with
the evidence of speaking in other tongues
(languages).

After a long, hard days work (I was
too weary to kneel) and simply stretched
out on the bedroom floor with hands
lifted in praise & worship, repeating
the awesome name of Jesus, and suddenly
He was there! I _saw_ + _felt_ Him lift
my sins, burdens and heartaches and
saw Him place them on His own shoulders.
Waves of love washed over me and I
reached to take the load back in order to
spare Him. He touched my uplifted hand
and I felt, as it were, His warm
precious blood flow down my hand
+ arm. For weeks + months following,
I would automatically hesitate to put
my hand into water because I didn't
want to wash away His blood!

Space does not allow me to tell of
the Shekinah Glory that filled that

room so many years ago as I began
speaking in a heavenly language.

I am still a "God-chaser" who
almost caught Him that night! The
above experience could be called a
"memorial" erected in the "River of
my Life" to remind me of His unfailing love + faithfulness, and to hold
me steady as I raised three "God-chasers"
alone.

Juanita (Frazier) Essert
January 2004

135

Mrs. Juanita Essert

My most profound encounter with our wonderful Lord was the night I was baptized in His Holy Spirit with the evidence of speaking in tongues (other languages).

After a long, hard day's work, I was too weary to kneel and simply stretched out on the bedroom floor with hands lifted in praise and worship, repeating the awesome name of Jesus, and suddenly **He** was there! I **saw** and **felt** Him lift my sins, burdens, and heartaches and saw Him place them on His own shoulders. Waves of love washed over me and I reached to take the load back in order to spare Him. He touched my uplifted hand and I felt, as it were, His warm, precious blood flow down my hand and arm. For weeks and months following, I would automatically hesitate to put my hand into water because I didn't want to wash away His blood!

Space does not allow me to tell of the Shekinah glory that filled that room, hallway, and into the other bedroom so many years ago as I began speaking in a heavenly language.

I am still a "God-chaser" who almost caught Him that night! The above experience could be called a "memorial" erected in the "River of My Life" to remind me of His unfailing love and faithfulness, and to hold me steady as I raised three "God-chasers" alone!

Juanita (Frazier) Essert
January 2004

Mrs. Juanita Essert
"Compassionate and gentle, a doer of the Word"

God sometimes communicates with Juanita Essert through pictures. For example, when she was rearing her children, a picture of the place where one of her children was at that moment would glide (like a moving picture show) through her head! As years passed and Mrs. Essert became an intercessor for her community and nation and the world, God used these pictures to impart an understanding of national events so that, having the heart of God, she and others could pray.

In 2004, when, by federal court order, workers were instructed to remove a 5,280-pound Ten Commandments granite monument that had been placed in the rotunda of the Alabama Supreme Court building by Chief Justice Roy Moore, God gave Juanita the following "encounter": *"Last week I was home alone, walking through the house. All was quiet—no TV, no music, no noise of any kind--when suddenly the presence of the Lord hit me so heavily I thought I was going to fall to the floor, and (since the 'human' is so present with us) I looked to see if I would hit the end of the coffee table. As I fell on my knees, I saw into another dimension: I saw the way God looked upon the removal of the Ten Commandments from the courthouse where Judge Roy Moore is/was involved. From God's point of view, He (God) was removed and the ropes actually dragged Him away. He didn't want to go but gave in to man's desire! As we watched on TV, it appeared His Words and His law were being removed (and they were), but it went much deeper than that. He (God) was leaving! AND, OH, THE DESOLATION OF A PLACE EMPTY OF HIS PRESENCE. I was reminded of how His presence left the temple in the Old Testament.*

"I had prayed and joined with others before this removal took place, but I now realize that passion for righteousness was lacking in my life and I know what God says about being lukewarm. Every Christian in this nation should have stood up and protested; the Church as a body should be involved in fasting and prayer to stop the removal of His name from the pledge, schools, and marriages. We're actually allowing the unrighteous to remove His name, and,

therefore, His presence and blessings from our nation. God forgive us! I am still amazed at the power of His presence that day and how important this situation in our nation is to Him!" ("*In the beginning was the Word, and the Word was with God, and the Word was God. In him was life, and that life was the light of men--John 1:1 & 4.*")

Mrs. Essert, as an Associate Pastor, has been involved in Women's Ministries and Prayer, Sunday school teacher, Bible teacher, director of in-home meetings, retreat organizer and speaker, and a board member of a local Christian high school.

To the mother of three adult Christian children she is still indispensable. (After her husband's early death she remained a "single" mom because "I didn't want to take the chance of a step-father mistreating my children.") To her five grandchildren she is the shoulder they cry on and the one who buys their lunch—even though they have good jobs; to her three great-grandchildren she is "granna"; to her friends she is gentle and has a sense of humor with laugher that can ease the tense atmosphere of any meeting, gathering, or phone call. Often praying at 3 a.m. to 5 a.m., she regularly visits those who are in prison, and, at odd hours, counsels young and old. If she senses something needs doing, she is the first one to get others started--and then she releases the cares of the day by reading _A Cat Who_ novel. She lives part time in the Colorado mountains and part time in Central California.

THE TEN COMMANDMENTS

"And God spoke all these words, saying:

1. You shall have no other gods before Me.
2. You shall not make for yourself a carved image—any likeness of anything that is in heaven above, or that is in the earth beneath, or that is in the water under the earth; you shall not bow down to them nor serve them. For I, the Lord your God, am a jealous God, visiting the iniquity of the fathers upon the children to the third and fourth generations of those who hate Me, but showing mercy to thousands, to those who love Me and keep My commandments.
3. You shall not take the name of the Lord your God in vain, for the Lord will not hold him guiltless who takes His name in vain.
4. Remember the Sabbath day, to keep it holy. Six days you shall labor and do all your work, but the seventh day is the Sabbath of the Lord your God. In it you shall do no work; you, nor your son, nor your daughter, nor your male servant, nor your female servant, nor your cattle, nor your stranger who is within your gates. For in six days the Lord made the heavens and the earth, the sea, and all that is in them, and rested the seventh day. Therefore the Lord blessed the Sabbath day and hallowed it.
5. Honor your father and your mother, that your days may be long upon the land which the Lord your God is giving you.
6. You shall not murder.

7. You shall not commit adultery.
8. You shall not steal.
9. You shall not bear false witness against your neighbor.
10. You shall not covet your neighbor's house; you shall not covet your neighbor's wife, nor his male servant, nor his female servant, nor his ox, nor his donkey, nor anything that is your neighbor's."

--Exodus 20:3-17

NEVER AGAIN will I confess "I can't," for *"I can do all things through Christ who strengthens me"* (Philippians 4:13).

NEVER AGAIN will I confess lack, for *"My God shall supply all of my need according to His riches in glory by Christ Jesus"* (Philippians 4:19).

NEVER AGAIN will I confess fear, for *"God hath not given me the spirit of fear, but of power, and of love, and of a sound mind"* (2 Timothy 1:7).

NEVER AGAIN will I confess doubt and lack of faith, for *"God hath given to every man the measure of faith"* (Romans 12:3).

NEVER AGAIN will I confess weakness, for *"The Lord is the strength of my life"* (Psalm 27:1) and *"The people that know their God shall be strong and do exploits"* (Daniel 11:32).

NEVER AGAIN will I confess supremacy of Satan over my life, for *"Greater is he that is within me than he that is in the world"* (1John 4:4).

NEVER AGAIN will I confess defeat, for *"God always causes me to triumph in Christ Jesus"* (2 Corinthians 2:14).

NEVER AGAIN will I confess lack of wisdom, for *"Christ Jesus is made unto me wisdom from God"* (1 Corinthians 1:30).

NEVER AGAIN will I confess sickness, for *"With His stripes I am healed"* (Isaiah 53:5), and Jesus *"Himself took my infirmities and bare my sicknesses"* (Matthew 8:17).

NEVER AGAIN will I confess worries and frustrations, for I am *"Casting all my cares upon him who careth for me"* (1 Peter 5:7). In Christ I am "care-free!"

NEVER AGAIN will I confess bondage, for *"Where the Spirit of the Lord is, there is liberty"* (2 Corinthians 3:17). My body is the temple of the Holy Spirit!

NEVER AGAIN will I confess condemnation, for *"There is therefore now no condemnation to them which are in Christ*

Jesus" **(Romans 8:1). I am in Christ; therefore, I am free from condemnation.**

--Don Gossett

In 1961 **God began dealing with our next participant** about the fact he had "developed a negative pattern of speech." He said he realized his "words were out of harmony with God's Word," that he was "disagreeing with the Lord when he said "I'm afraid' and God said, "Fear not." **Further, he realized what is meant in Amos 3:3 as the question was asked, "Can two walk together, except they be agreed?" He realized he needed to say what God said about health, finances, strength, anointing, and blessings promised in His Word.**

As a result, Rev. Gossett began writing in his diary for his "own admonition" the NEVER AGAIN LIST. The list was printed in several books and has gone around the world. (Used with permission.)

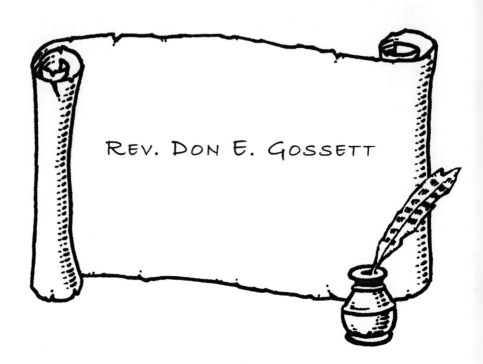

REV. DON E. GOSSETT

My name is Don Gisett. I was
born in Oklahoma to non-Christian parents.
I was introduced to Jesus at age 12, and
received Him as my Saviour and Lord.

At 17 I was called by the Lord to prepare
to preach the Gospel. Being filled with the Holy
Spirit was a deep life-changing experience,
with the evidence of speaking in tongues.

Writing books, 112 of them, broadcasting
by radio into 89 nations, going personally
to 55 countries for crusades — these have
been my highlights.

The delight of being married to two different
women (first one deceased) and having five children
and 12 grandchildren have crowned my life
with supreme joy.

I am eternally grateful for Jesus,

Don E. Gisett
P.O. Box 2
Blaine, WA, 98231

145

DON E.GOSSETT

www.dongossett.com

My name is Don Gossett. I was born in Oklahoma to non-Christian parents. I was introduced to Jesus at age 12, and received Him as my Saviour and Lord.

At 17 I was called by the Lord to prepare to preach the Gospel. Being filled with the Holy Spirit was a deep life-changing experience, with the evidence of speaking in tongues.

Writing books, 112 of them, broadcasting by radio into 89 nations, going personally to 55 countries for crusades—these have been my highlights.

The delight of being married to two different women (first one deceased) and having five children and 12 grandchildren have crowned my life with supreme joy.

I am eternally grateful for Jesus,

Don E. Gossett
P.O. Box 2
Blaine, WA 98231

REVEREND DON GOSSETT

Proverbs 27:21 states "*…a man is valued by what others say of him.*" One of the greatest accomplishments for a parent, wrote Judy Gossett, is "*to have their own flesh and blood actively involved with the parent, endorsing them, believing in and wholeheartedly supporting the work God has called their fathers to.*" In her father's book **The Power of Your Words**, Judy, the oldest daughter, paid the highest tribute (on behalf of five Gossett children) to her father, Don Gossett:

She told of memories she had when the family traveled from one evangelistic service to another, of the bonding that took place as they listened to Bible stories, as they memorized Scripture, as they played together outside a motel room. She told also of the "*near-poverty, sickness, mediocrity and frustration*" until 1961 when God revealed to her dad that "**the power of <u>Jesus' name</u> coupled with the positive <u>confession</u> of the Word and joyful <u>praise</u> were the keys to success and victorious living.**" The entire family knew from experience the revolution that occurred in their family! We "*never again lived in the defeatism of past years in the ministry.*" She called Rev. Gossett "*compassionate man of God, loving father, proud grandfather,*" and her "*wonderful friend.*"

Our generation remembers Rev. Don Gossett for his "bold Bible teaching" about praise, about the power of our words, and about right confession based on the Word of God. We remember him not for a "name it and claim it" charade but for teaching us about "The Great Confession" (Christianity **is** called 'The Great Confession') as found in Hebrews 4:14,16: "*Seeing then that we have a great High Priest who has passed through the heavens, Jesus the Son of God, let us hold fast our confession…. Let us therefore come boldly to the throne of grace, that we may obtain mercy and find grace to help in time of need.*" Rev. Gossett inspired us to believe that the Word takes the place of Jesus in our lives, and "**We are to obey the Word as we would obey Jesus if He stood in our presence.**" To begin confessing the Word, means to begin possessing the things we have confessed based on the Living Word of God, not on a philosophy or on our own mental will. And that fact makes all the difference!

In 1961, Gossett was challenged by a man to *"talk the way you would like to be and you will be the way you talk."* He had just had his house and furniture repossessed and he and his family were living in two small rooms in a motel.

He began to affirm statements such as "God gives me wealth and health" based on God's Word. *"Beloved, I wish above all things that you may prosper and be in health, even as your soul prospers--*(3 John 2:1)." He began to confess, *"My God shall supply all my need according to His riches in glory by Christ Jesus"*--Philippians 4:19. He disciplined his "lips and held" his "heart steady" for the supply of a home, ***but most of all, for a ministry that would enable me to be an achiever in Jesus, a positive help to poverty-shackled, fettered and oppressed people."***

Again, his source for declarations was the Word of God since Jesus had declared in John 6:63, *"It is the Spirit who gives life; the flesh profits nothing. **The words that I speak unto you, they are spirit and they are life.**"* Hebrews 4:12 records that *"For the **Word of God is living and powerful** and sharper than any two-edged sword, piercing even to the division of soul and spirit, and of joints and marrow, and is a discerner of the thoughts and intents of the heart."* Gossett spoke God's word aloud over and over and over.

He began talking like an achiever, *"I shall utilize the modern communication's methods to preach the Gospel. I shall succeed as a radio broadcaster. The Holy Spirit has put many books into my heart. I shall write those books."* He continued talking his way forward, confessing the Word, and refusing negative confessions. From failure in almost every thing he had done, he eventually became the way he talked. And yes, he and his family did get the house!

Born again at age 12, Don Gossett answered the Lord's call five years later to spread the Gospel. His first goal was to win his own unbelieving family members to Christ. Even as a teen-aged Bible college student, Don often preached anywhere people would listen-- parks, street corners, and small churches. An unusual anointing to help others increased, and we feel this anointing as it permeates his books and broadcasts.

In classics such as *What You Say Is What You Get*, *The Power of Your Words*, and *The power of Spoken Faith*, Rev. Gossett pioneered the way in writing truths about the power of the spoken word. Translated into eighteen languages, his books now exceed 25 million in worldwide distribution. His daily radio broadcast, launched in 1961 called "Bold Bible Living," has been released in eighty-nine nations. For years he kept "teaching cards" of inspiration he received from the Word. Now he places these teaching lessons on his Website (www.dongossett.com) under "daily devotional". As a missionary evangelist, he has ministered in 55 nations with signs and wonders following the Word of God. He has been in full-time ministry for fifty-seven years as of 2005—that is a story of Spirit-directed success!

To excel, an athlete hires a trainer or coach; to succeed as an electrician a person becomes an apprentice to a master electrician; to succeed in any area of life a person needs a mentor. Rev. Gossett found himself under the influence of great leaders of faith. **First,** he learned from his wife Joyce about the power of praise. *"The Holy Spirit stripped away the inhibitions that kept me from praising Jesus without embarrassment."* In the book *There's Dynamite In Praise,* (listed as a "classic" in most bookstores) he tells about the new joy he found in learning to praise God. One hundred Bible verses relating to the importance of praise are listed in the book, and he encourages us to memorize them and to begin praising God!

Not only when all is going well, but even when we do not feel like it, we are to offer the sacrifice of praise to God. **Praise is not optional for a Christian**. We praise to glorify God, not man. Psalm 50:23 declares, *"Whoever offers praise glorifies Me;...* Praise is **to be done aloud** as Psalm 66:8 reminds us: *"Oh, bless our God, you peoples! And make the voice of His praise to be heard,...."* *"Obedience to praise brings victorious living!"*

One woman who received the message of praise began shouting "hallelujah" to the refrigerator each time she passed it. God miraculously started bringing food (by way of people) to the house to feed her family. The Lord *"inhabits the praises of his people-- (Psalm 22:3)."* Gossett says, *"Wise is the Christian who discerns his trouble to be satanic and then employs the power of praise against the Devil."*

Second, Rev. Gossett learned from William Freeman, Jack Coe, and T.L. Osborne, and discovered the power of **praying in the name of Jesus**. Starting out as a Baptist minister, he later spent five years "as an apprentice" with William W. Freeman (a man who held large tent meetings where thousands were saved and healed). Later Gossett worked as a writer for the evangelist Jack Coe. In 1959-60 he was editor of T. L. Osborn's magazine <u>Faith Digest</u>. **He witnessed in all these ministries the power and authority of the name of Jesus** as nations were stirred by the gospel. Rev. Gossett said **he prayed to be able to have that kind of ministry and power**. Finally, one morning while he was praying, the Holy Spirit "poured a staggering revelation" into him. The Holy Spirit spoke through Philippians 2:9-11: *"Therefore God also has highly exalted Him [Jesus] and given Him the name which is above every name, that **at the name of Jesus every knee should bow**, of those in heaven, and of those on earth, and of those under the earth, and that **every tongue should confess that Jesus Christ is Lord, to the glory of God the Father.**"* That was the secret: praying in the name of Jesus!

After meeting a hitchhiker who said he had always wanted to be a Christian but said he couldn't be, Rev. Gossett was troubled. Then the Holy Spirit revealed to him how satan blinds minds and eyes to the truth. He quietly said, *"Devil, **in the name of Jesus**, take your hands off this man. He desires salvation from Jesus Christ, and you have deceived him long enough."* Suddenly the man turned to Gossett and said, *"I am ready to pray."* That incident surprised Gossett but caused him to realize the authority Jesus has given to us.

Rev. Gossett has commanded Satan's power to be broken off of lives in whole groups and even large audiences of unsaved people. In services where people stand stoically without response to an invitation to accept Jesus Christ, Rev. Gossett will pray, *"Devil, **in the name of Jesus**, take your hands off this congregation. They desire salvation from Jesus Christ, and you have deceived them long enough."* Suddenly people begin moving forward for salvation. Through the years thousands have come to Jesus in his crusades and thousands have been healed. *"As we use Jesus name we know He is alive. We may not see Him but He backs up our commands."*

When he prayed with the hitchhiker, Gossett said, *"I saw Jesus in His name that night."*

His **third** mentoring program was with the Holy Spirit and Scripture. In 1961, God quoted Scripture to Rev. Gossett: "First He said, '*You have wearied the Lord with your words* (Malachi 2:17). *Your words have been stout against Me*, says the Lord. (Malachi 3:13).'" Gossett said he was shocked! Then the Holy Spirit brought to his attention that he had developed a negative pattern of speech using phrases like "I can't," and "I'm afraid." *"My words were not in harmony with God's Word; I was disagreeing with the Lord when His Word told me "I can," and "Fear not."*

At that time of "reproof," Rev. Gossett wrote in his diary a "**Never Again List**" which has been published many times and shared with people worldwide. It is true, he says that "*if you believe what you are saying, What You Say Is What You Get.*"

For a long time Gossett said he was confused over the fact that in his own life and in the lives of so many others there was a "continual sense of defeat and failure." One day while reading Hebrews 4:14 he saw that "we are to hold fast to our **confession**." He wondered, "What confession?" *"Hold fast to my confession of the absolute integrity of the Bible...of the redemptive work of Christ...of receiving the life and nature of God...that God is the strength of my life...that by His stripes I am healed...that God supplies every need of mine."*

He admonishes us to study the Word until we know what our rights are and then hold fast to those rights—based on the Word of God. *"It's important to understand that What You Say* **Is** *What you Get, not because your words themselves have power, but because* **your own words make it possible for God's power to work on your behalf."**

Rev. Gossett calls his idea "*The Speaking Forth Principle, the very ingredient of faith.*" When we confess Jesus as Lord "unto salvation" (Romans 10:10), then God acts to recreate our spirit. *"When a sinner is converted, first, he* **believes** *on the Lord Jesus Christ and that God raised Him from the dead; then his* **confession** *is made unto salvation."* Just as God spoke the Word first and His acts of creation came into being, so it is **in every situation;** the follower of Christ is to speak, and then he will possess. *"God fulfills all His promises the same way."*

151

Numerous healings have taken place in Rev. Gossett's meetings, but healings began first in his own life and family. When his first wife, Joyce, was bedridden with rheumatic fever, "...*The Lord is the strength of my life...*" (based on Psalm 27:1) was "quickened" to Gossett and after Joyce began repeating the verse, slowly but daily her strength returned and she began walking again.

In a recent newsletter Gossett told of a serious auto accident he and a friend were in. Don walked away unhurt, but his friend was taken to a hospital in critical condition. At one point the minister friend asked Don to go to a room to pray for he believed because the pain was so severe, he would not make it through the night. Early the next morning Don returned, found the bed empty, and began to weep knowing his friend had died. About that time, the friend walked out of the bathroom, clothed, and healed. He said in his near-death experience, Jesus told him to return to finish the work He had for him! An interesting remark the minister made was "dying was the happiest day of my life!"

Healing, Rev. Gossett reminds us, is not something that will come about if we say words, or if we pray. It is something that has **already** been done! Just as we were saved the minute we accepted the atonement of Jesus on the cross, so we can be healed the minute we really see that Jesus has already paid the price for our healing. "*If you are God's child, you must say what the Bible says in order to get the results the Bible promises.*"

Don's first wife Joyce went to be with the Lord in 1991. They had five children who have all served the Lord and helped in his ministry. Son Michael is often heard on the radio broadcast. Judy joined her mother in heaven in 2003. In 1995, Rev. Gossett married Debra and together they continue ministering around the globe as a husband and wife team. Headquartered in Blaine, Washington, he has eleven grandchildren and one great grandchild.

.

"Therefore you shall lay up these words of Mine
in your heart and in your soul,
and bind them as a sign on your hand,
and they shall be as frontlets between your eyes.
You shall teach them to your children,
speaking of them when you sit in your house,
when you walk by the way,
when you lie down, and when you rise up.
And you shall write them on the doorposts
of your house and on your gates,
<u>that your days and the days</u>
<u>of your children may be multiplied</u>
in the land of which the Lord swore to your
fathers to give them, like the days of the heavens
above the earth."

--Deuteronomy 11:18-21

"For We Do Not Wrestle Against Flesh And Blood,

but against principalities, against powers, against the rulers of the darkness of this age, against spiritual hosts of wickedness in the heavenly places." -- Ephesians 6:12

"All of us engaged in Christian work are constantly aware of the fact that we have to do battle with supernatural forces and powers....
It is perfectly obvious to all of us in spiritual work that people can be possessed by demons, harassed by them and controlled by them. More and more ministers will have to learn to use the power of God to release people from these terrible possessions by the devil."
—Dr. Billy Graham

Our next participant pioneered the way in teaching our generation about spiritual warfare:

Testimony

convinces

others

about

God's

reality!

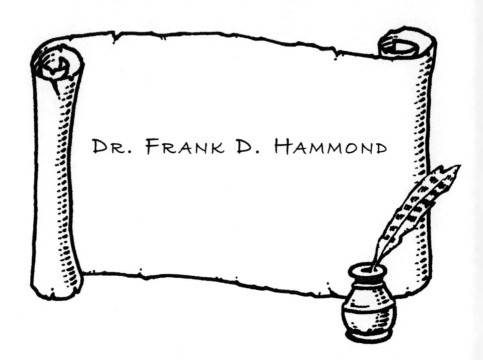

DR. FRANK D. HAMMOND

THE CHILDREN'S BREAD MINISTRY

Frank D. Hammond

PO Box 789, Plainview, TX 79073

February 28, 2004

Stable personalities are the products of stable families. I am blessed beyond measure to have had Christian parents who brought me up "in the nurture and admonition of the Lord". My father, Joseph Carroll Hammond, II, read the Bible and had prayer with the family at the breakfast table each day. When I was yet a small child, through a weekly allowance of ten cents, he taught me to always give a tenth to the Lord.

I am also blessed to have had a good wife, Ida Mae Loden. We were married forty-nine years before her death in 1997. She had a call of God on her life and was a strong woman of God. For twenty years I was a pastor with her at my side. Then, Jesus appeared in our bedroom one night and called me by name. At first, we could not imagine what another call would be. I had been called to salvation at ten years of age; called to the ministry at age twenty-six and called into the baptism in the Holy Spirit at age forty-five. We were soon to discover that this new call was to deliverance ministry. God thrust us into deliverance, and for several years we were in a school of the Holy Spirit, learning from the Word and personal experience the basics of setting the captives free.

In 1973, our first book was published: *Pigs In The Parlor, A Practical Guide to Deliverance*. This book carries a special anointing and eventually became listed in the top ten best seller according to Charisma Magazine. Within thirty years it exceeded one million copies in print and published in sixteen languages. We taught and ministered deliverance in churches, camps and conferences throughout the United States.

In 1980, the Lord began to open doors of opportunity for us in other nations, so that we left the pastorate to be engaged in an international ministry, traveling to sixteen countries and four continents. Our teaching and ministry emphasis was deliverance and family relationships.

Our ministry became known as "The Children's Bread", taken from Mark 5:27 where deliverance from demon spirits is called "the children's bread". This ministry is an outreach of New Covenant Church, Plainview, Texas.

As I look back on my life, I am awed by God's faithfulness. No wonder my favorite hymn is: "Great is thy faithfulness, O God my Father. There is no shadow of turning with thee; Thou changest not, thy compassions, they fail not; as Thou has been Thou forever will be. Pardon for sin and a peace that endureth. Thine own dear presence to cheer and to guide; strength for today and bright hope for tomorrow. Blessings all mine, with ten thousand beside! Great is thy faithfulness! Great is thy faithfulness! Morning by morning new mercies I see; all I have needed Thy hand hath provided; great is Thy faithfulness, Lord, unto me."— (Written by Thomas O. Chisholm, 1923).

Frank Davis Hammond

Dr. Frank D. Hammond

His desire was to set the captive free!

After the 1973 publication of his first book, as mentioned in his testimony, Dr. Hammond wrote at least eight more books on deliverance. **Our generation** remembers him for taking a bold stand in encouraging the Church to become more involved in setting captives free.

Born in Texas, Frank Hammond received his B.A. degree from Baylor University and a B.D. degree from Southwestern Theological Seminary in Fort Worth, Texas, becoming an ordained Baptist minister. He served as a "city pastor" for twenty years, but "became hungry for personal revival." To fulfill the quest of something more spiritually satisfying, he left for a season of "resort mission work" in the ski areas of Colorado. After Hammond had a series of personal encounters with the Lord, he says, *"Jesus appeared in my bedroom one night and called me by name."* It was a call to the ministry of spiritual warfare.

For the next six years Frank was in the school of the Holy Spirit where he was taught the principles of spiritual warfare and deliverance. Based on Joel 2:28 *("...I will pour out My spirit on all flesh...Your old men shall dream dreams; your young men shall see visions."),* he also asked God for visions, a request God granted many times in his life. (One of his booklets *God Warns America* was a result.) He realized God was calling him to an entirely different ministry, a ministry of **teaching people how to "resist the devil."** *("Therefore, submit to God. Resist the devil and he will flee from you."* James 4:7) He and his wife taught and ministered throughout the United States, Canada, Europe, South America, and behind the Iron Curtain. They began conducting **family seminars** and wrote the book *Kingdom Living For The Family.*

Hammond believed the church and the individual must get to the concept of doing spiritual warfare against the spiritual rulers who are called "the spiritual hosts of wickedness in heavenly places." Ephesians 6:10-12 records, *"Finally, my brethren, be strong in the Lord and in the power of His might. Put on the whole armor of God, that you may be able to stand against the wiles of the devil. For we do not wrestle against flesh and blood, but against principalities, against powers, against the rulers of the darkness of this age, against spiritual hosts of wickedness in the heavenly places."*

He was quick to point out that demons cannot possess or have ownership of a Christian *"because he is owned by Christ,"* but demons may trespass. He said Christians must recognize Satan is a defeated foe stripped of his power and his kingdom. It is up to the Christian to defend his rights and seriously desire him [satan] to go. We have every right to treat satan as a trespasser.

The popularity of *Pigs In The Parlor* is revealed by the fact that in 2003 it went into its 38th printing. The book is still found in stores; it is used as a guide in several Christian college courses; and we discovered it to be recommended reading on a Website dealing with mental disturbances such as Schizophrenia. A lengthy discussion is included in one chapter where Hammond tells how God revealed that many people in our society have dual personalities. God showed him that the core of many of these problems is **Rejection** and **Rebellion.** To anyone involved in counseling, ministering, or intercessory prayer, we recommend the chapter.

Dr. Hammond explains that twenty-five times in the New Testament demons are called "unclean spirits," and the same word "unclean" is used to designate certain creatures, such as the pig, that the Israelite was not supposed to eat or touch--hence, the title *Pigs In The Parlor.*

Hammond taught that just as the Israelite protected himself from contact with pigs, the Christian is to guard himself from contact with evil spirits. In the same way we would deal with pigs coming into our house (our parlor), Christians are to immediately drive out evil spirits as soon as they are discovered. Our bodies are the temples of the Holy Spirit and we should permit nothing to defile that temple.

Hammond often quoted **Billy Graham** as saying, ***"It is perfectly obvious to all of us in spiritual work that people can be possessed by demons, harassed by them and controlled by them. More and more ministers will have to learn to use the power of God to release people from these terrible possessions by the devil."*** Hammond said that he was astonished by the number of people who came forward in his meetings asking to be ministered to. *"They come because* *they are already reaching out to God. They are believers who want to continue in spiritual growth and realize that every hindrance to spiritual development must be eliminated."*

Hammond explains the practical application of the ministry of deliverance, patterned after the ministry of Jesus Christ. (All four Gospels record the event of Jesus cleansing the temple.) Jesus was filled with righteous indignation at what he found in the temple and began to purge the temple of every defiling thing—*"an illustration of the cleansing of our bodies, which are temples of the Holy Spirit."*

The Bible refers to curses over 230 times and 70 sins that cause curses. Curses are just as real today as in Biblical times, and Dr. Hammond shows what they are and how to deliver yourself and your family from them. Other closely related ideas he taught were the following:

1) Demons afflict the emotions, the mind, the will, and the physical body—not the spirit of a Christian.

2) The remedy for rejection is forgiveness, repentance, and prayers for deliverance.

3) Often deliverance is needed for children because of the dangers inherent in the influence of certain toys, games, music, and television.

4) Pray for cities and for nations--each Christian is a soldier, equipped with spiritual weapons to engage in spiritual warfare.

5) The power of binding and loosing are two keys by which we defeat satan's kingdom (Matthew 16:19).

6) Start with yourself! ***"Personal deliverance is the starting point for total spiritual warfare; the first objective is to free oneself."*** Demons talk to our minds (like telling us a friend thinks we are stupid) planting seeds of resentment and suspicion.

Hammond says to speak out loud and say something like: *"You are a liar, demon. I reject that thought about my friend. My mind is under the protection of the blood of Jesus. I bind you from my thoughts. I command you to leave me alone, in the name of Jesus."* That is resisting the devil, for he often uses negative thinking to get a fix or stronghold on our minds. Find the area in your life where you know demons are troubling you, and command them to come out in Jesus' name. Do not let them go unchallenged another day! *"...for the kingdom of God is...righteousness and peace and joy in the Holy Spirit"* (Romans 14:17). This is God's inheritance for you NOW! It is yours for the taking!

"Warfare is not prayer! It is an addition to prayer. There is no point in petitioning God for something He has already given you. God has given us power and authority over the devil. Spiritual warfare on behalf of another **does not control the will of that person. It binds the power of demon forces and releases the will** *to make decisions apart from demon interference. Demons are not cast out of the person, but their power is bound for a season."*

In one place Hammond pastored, he was given a vision of the "prince spirit" over the community. The vision revealed a large, octopus-like creature hovering over the city. Across its head was written "Jealousy." Its tentacles reached down and were entwining and crushing every facet of community life—churches, schools, businesses, homes, social life, government, recreation and personal relationships. God showed him that the tentacles represented strife, criticism, envy, backbiting, greed, gossip, selfishness and covetousness.

Demons are enemies of the gifts and fruits of the Spirit. The demon of doubt or unbelief can block the flow of faith and thereby block the flow of prophecy. Deal with the hindering spirits, Hammond says. The demon of resentment can defeat love in a person's life. Resentment usually invites in other demons, such as bitterness, hatred and anger. *"The demon of the spirit of rejection must be cast out before that person can mature in Christian love."* Deal with them before they become strongholds.

How do demons enter? They can enter through life's circumstances (such as mistreatment as a child), through inheritance, or through sins of omission and commission (works of the flesh including adultery, fornication, pornography, television and movies (watching violence or fear-filled programs), sinister songs and music, witchcraft, cults, horoscopes, hatred, wrath, strife, envying, murders and drunkenness, etc). A classic example of the door being opened by the sin of omission is the failure to forgive.

"Christians can change the course of events in lives, families, communities, and nations by learning to bind the demonic spirits, loose them from their assignments, and cast them out."

Though he and his wife Ida ministered to large crowds, it was Dr. Hammond's custom to have conferences with individuals; they liked to schedule 2-hour sessions and **meet with an entire family.**

Satan's tactic is to **put pressure on us** in our thought life, in our emotions, in our decision-making, and in our physical bodies. Using tactics like a wrestler, *"God suggests the remedy for victory over demonic pressures is spiritual warfare."* Ephesians 6:12 tells us we are fighting against "principalities"—literally things in a series; a series of leaders or rulers describe their demonic rank and organization. The ruling spirits are assigned over areas such as nations and cities as borne out by Daniel's prayer being stopped in the heavenlies. The angel explained, *"The prince of the kingdom of Persia had hindered him."* (Daniel 10) Dr. Hammond said, *"Problems that persist and plague churches and homes and individuals may well indicate that special evil agents have been assigned to cause trouble."*

The demons have power (Luke 10:19—*"Behold, I give you the authority to trample...over all the **power of the enemy**"*....).

The believer has greater authority than the demonic agents! Demons are forced to yield to the authority of the name of Jesus. *"And these signs shall follow those who believe: IN MY NAME they shall cast out demons;"*....Mark 16:17. Dr. Hammond emphasized the importance of Acts 1:8: *"But you shall receive power, after that the Holy Spirit is come upon you."* Hammond stated it would be *"sheer folly to go against demon spirits without this power and authority. The authority comes through salvation; the power comes through the baptism in the Holy Spirit. The power given the believer through the mighty baptism in the Holy Spirit is evidenced through the operation of the gifts of the Spirit (I Corinthians 12:7-11). Such gifts of the Spirit as supernatural words of knowledge and discerning of spirits are indispensable in spiritual warfare. This power and the authority of Jesus' name are given that the believer might overcome demon powers."*

Why do so many people shun the thought or conversation that it is possible to be under demonic influence?

Could it be because demons do not want to be exposed and, thus, they cause men to resist the thought or conversation about them?

Why do conversations become hushed when the gifts of the Holy Spirit are mentioned?

Could it be because the operation of these supernatural gifts of power counters the work of demons and, thus, demons strongly oppose the gifts?

In November 2004, after having a stroke, Frank Hammond passed away. It was just February 2004, when he sent his typed story with a note explaining that he could no longer provide a handwritten encounter but that he could still type! **"Would I please include him in the project?"** At various times during the gathering of the material, the recorder was tempted to quit, **but for Frank Hammond!** For his sake, if for no other reason, I was driven to complete the project. I choose to believe that somewhere in heaven Dr. Hammond knows that he is being honored and **remembered by our generation** for his obedience to our Heavenly Father--for his research and teaching and ministry to people, bringing deliverance to those who are harassed or made captive by demonic activity!

*"Through the Lord's mercies we are not consumed, because His compassions fail not. They are new every morning; **Great is Your faithfulness**. 'The Lord is my portion,' says my soul, therefore I hope in Him! The Lord is good to those who wait for Him, to the soul who seeks Him—Lamentations 3:22-25."*

"...Set your hearts on all the words which I testify among you today, which you shall command your children to be careful to observe—all the words of this law. For it is not a futile thing for you because it is your life, and by this word you shall prolong your days in the land which you cross over the Jordan to possess."

--Deuteronomy 32:46-47

"There are very few in their hearts who do not believe in God, but what they will not do is give Him exclusive right-of-way. They are not ready to promise full allegiance to God alone."—D. L. Moody

****

HOW TO LIVE A TOTALLY COMMITTED, SURRENDERED, ABANDONED LIFE FOR JESUS CHRIST

--Madam Guyon

"There must enter into your heart whole new attitudes toward your entire life. It is required that you begin to abandon your whole existence, giving it up to God. You must believe that the circumstances of your life, that is, every minute of your life, as well as the whole course of your life—anything, yes, everything that happens—have all come to you by His will and by His permission. You must believe that everything that has happened to you is from God and is exactly what you need.

"Abandonment, or total surrender, is casting all your cares. Abandonment is dropping all your needs. This includes spiritual needs. Abandonment is forgetting your past; it is leaving the future in His hands; it is devoting the present fully and completely to your Lord. Abandonment is being satisfied with the present moment, no matter what that moment contains. You are satisfied because you know that whatever that moment has, it contains—in that instant—God's eternal plan for you. Surrender not only what the Lord does to you, but surrender your reaction to what He does. (Remember, you must never blame man for anything. No matter what happens, it was neither man nor circumstances that brought it.) Accept everything (**except, of course, your own sinfulness**) as having come from your Lord. That is surrender."

****

Our next participants have learned to live by the words from Galatians 2:20:

"I have been crucified with Christ; it is no longer I who live, but Christ lives in me; and the life which I now live in the flesh I live by faith in the Son of God, who loved me and gave Himself for me."

MRS. ANITA HASHIM

A Vow Not Kept!

Mrs. Anita Hashim
www.MannaFromOnHigh.com

At sixteen years of age I found Christ as my Savior at a youth camp. For a year or more I had observed the woman who led me to the Lord, because with total humility, she lived a life of entire commitment to Christ. When she prayed, God answered and I had the utmost confidence that she knew Christ intimately. She became my living example of what living for Christ should be, and I intended to follow her example.

My family thought my dedication to God was a good thing, but something I would have to do without attending church on Sunday because they had other plans for their weekends. It was then that I knew total commitment was out of the question, so I made a vow to God. I told God that if He would protect me until I had a home of my own that I would totally commit my life to Him.

Seven years passed and I was totally aware that I had enjoyed God's protection and some marvelous blessings. I was twenty-three and had been married for two years. Then I became very ill and the doctors couldn't cure my lung infections, and I lost our first child. I coughed continuously and my breathing could be heard across the room. Nothing helped me! Finally, one day I felt like going outside and sitting in the sun. I was still no better. I sat on a stool and thought of my hopeless situation. Suddenly, I heard a voice within me saying, "I kept my part of your vow, but you have not kept yours." Then I heard God say, "If I depart from you today, how will you ever come to Me?"

I jumped up and ran into the house and fell before the couch and began to repent and make my vows of **total commitment** to God. I did not mean that I would live a Christian life to the best of my ability; I meant that Christ would be my life and He would come before everything else. I did not mean that I would make my decisions according to my desires but according to His word. In large decisions I vowed to look to him for His wisdom and divine help. I promised to walk daily with Him and not to fulfill the desires of my own flesh. I freely gave up my love for reading (secular fiction) and promised to read His word and to pray daily.

Instantly, the thought came to me that my husband was not going to like his new wife. I told the Lord, "My husband will divorce me." He replied, "I will never allow your marriage to be broken." He further said, "If you will walk uprightly before Me, I will divide with you the good of the land."—Isaiah 1:19

I got up from prayer and the whole world seemed new and I was filled with joy. Two or three days later I discovered that I was totally healed. God has more than kept His word to me and I have kept mine! I have had many experiences with the faithfulness of God and the abundance of life in Christ. I have proved His words to me over and over again. My life has been filled with supernatural workings of the Lord and ministries I would never had a part in if I had chosen my own path. There is nothing in this world to compare with daily intimacy with God and being His intercessor and witness. As it is written, "No eye has seen, no ear has heard, no mind has conceived what God has prepared for those who love him."

--I Corinthians 2:9

In Christ's Love,

Anita Harbison

MRS. ANITA HASHIM
"A woman who hears from God"

An unusual person (fun-loving but serious about Jesus Christ) is Mrs. Anita Hashim. (After opening a birthday present, she has been known to put the ribbons and wrapping on her head as a hat.) She secretly nibbles on mini-Butterfinger candy bars and peppermint ice cream. She is intelligent, sharp-of-mind, loves to tease her grandchildren and relax at her daughter's beach house.

Seemingly comfortable as a recluse with her Australian shepherd and her Bible, she is just as comfortable speaking to a group or setting the pace at a party. She is gentle but straightforward as a tiger! After going out for an evening meal, she might invite you into her home, not to watch television or play a game or drink tea or coffee (although she can be the perfect, attending hostess), **but to pray**!

As a prayer partner, the other person may never know what to expect since Mrs. Hashim often delivers prophetic messages or words of knowledge. In the midst of praying, one learns to wait for a signal to leave, because at times she may say, *"God is speaking."* She will then pick up a pen, begin to write, and you know to sit quietly. She says, *"I've learned to listen and obey when the Lord speaks."*

In our strident age of noise it is difficult to present the idea of silence before God, but much of Mrs. Hashim's communion with God is done in a quiet manner. *"God spoke to me once, when I was trying to pray as loudly as the others in the room, and said, 'You cannot hear Me when you are praying like that. The effort of the self must be stilled. The human will has to be put to rest. Then you will hear from Me'."* When Mrs. Hashim does not know how to pray in a given situation, she often prays in her heavenly language (to which the Apostle Paul referred—1 Corinthians 14:2); she says it is good to combine audible prayer with silent prayer.

And Mrs. Hashim's prayers are answered! She practices absolute trust and persevering faith in God in every circumstance in her life and in prayers for other people. She doesn't just possess faith; faith possesses her. She takes God without any "if." If God says it, she believes it. Thus, her faith in God carries her, and her faith in His Word causes prayer to work. Is it any wonder that, after attending a church service with Mrs. Hashim, the recorder was asked by another person, ***"Is that the woman who hears from God?"***

Through the years she has been led to have a number of prayer ministries and, for a time, held regular meetings at the YWCA. People have flown in from various places in the United States for prayer. When one minister made an appointment to bring his wife for prayer, everyone, including Mrs. Hashim, was surprised when God said, *"It is not the wife; it is the minister you are to pray for!"*

The mother of two children, one adopted son, and three grandchildren, Anita Hashim's early life was difficult and lacking in earthly love. She never recalls hearing her mother express any kind of love toward her. Even so, she said, *"I always knew, without going to church or to Sunday School, that God loved me and that I was special to Him!"* At the age of nine, when she knew nothing about Jesus Christ, she said God spoke to her to go to her bedroom, kneel and pray. God instructed her to ask Him to deliver her from her alcoholic mother. Following God's instructions, she prayed and a short time later her mother left. As a result, Anita was divinely placed with a family who were good to her though they seldom attended church. Thus (as already told in her entry), when Anita gave her heart to the Lord Jesus Christ at 16 years of age, she promised God that when she had her own home she would totally commit her life to Him if He would keep her and watch over her.

She and her husband, Vince, were successful for years in the supermarket business; however, much to the consternation of some in the community, God said, *"Remove the booze and put a Christian bookstore in that section!"* Her husband even set up a prayer room in one market so people could pray! Though they traveled extensively, the earlier commitment, which someone said became like a Nazarite vow, led Mrs. Hashim down a different path—a path of studying the Scripture, praying, being a friend of God, and having **Hebrews Chapter 11-like faith** *("...who through faith subdued kingdoms, wrought righteousness, obtained promises, **stopped the mouths of lions**,...")*. Mrs. Hashim is totally sold on Jesus Christ as Lord, and He, likewise, has showered His attention on her.

But, suffering from illnesses and family trials has sliced through her life. Undaunted, optimistic, determined, and never double-minded, she says she is victorious *"because of an awareness at all times that Christ dwells within me and that nothing, absolutely nothing, happens outside His will. We need to stress the fact,"* she says, *"that Jesus Christ dwells within a person, not out in space somewhere."*

No doubt because she has suffered so much, God has given Mrs. Hashim compassion for those who are suffering. God spoke to her in 2004 to start a website so He could *"speak to the lonely and disillusioned, the ones who have no anchor for their lives and are drifting aimlessly.... You have proven the answer in your own life—a life in Me controlled by My spirit."* She also conducts an intercessory prayer group called "The Burden Bearers."

Mrs. Hashim now uses her prayer anointing and prophetic calling to minister to people through the website (MannaFromOnHigh.com). Since God told her He would bring people to the site, she does not advertise; she remains in the background, and God **does** send people for prayer and deliverance. Her *"great love in Christ and the Father was and is intercession for souls, inner healings, and healing from sickness."* Amazingly, Mrs. Hashim and her granddaughter pray over each e-mail and return a personal answer given by God.

Because of her insistence on death to pride and giving God glory, that He only should be praised, Mrs. Hashim hesitated in approving some of the above material. **However, future generations will be blessed if they know that God can speak to an unchurched child (<u>even tell that child what to pray</u>) and then protect the child. Present and future generations appreciate and are encouraged to see and hear how God makes a surrendered life complete, fulfilling, and beautiful!**

"For to me, to live is Christ, and to die is gain."
Philippians 1:21

"...for in Him we live and move and have our being,....."
Acts 17:28

"Finally, brethren, whatever things are true,
whatever things are noble,
whatever things are just,
whatever things are pure,
whatever things are lovely,
if there is any virtue and if there is anything
praiseworthy--meditate on these things.
The things which you learned
and received and heard and saw in me,
these do, and the God of peace will be with you."
--Philippians 4:8-9

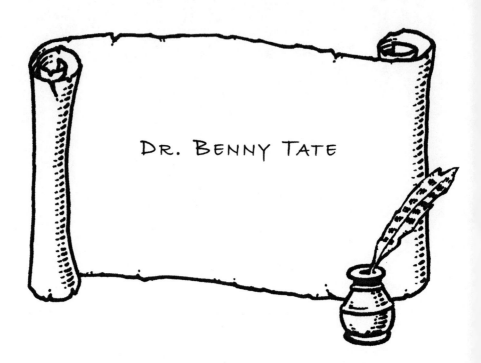

Dr. Benny Tate

If God Builds It, They Will Come

Not Equal Gifts, But Equal Sacrifice

A Proud Heritage,
Building on Faith
Through . . .

- Prayer

- Worship
  and the Word

- Fellowship

- Personal
  Commitment

Rock Springs
Congregational
Methodist Church
Dr. Benny Tate, Senior Pastor

219 Rock Springs Road
Milner, Georgia 30257
Phone: 770-229-8663
Fax: 770-229-6126
Web: rocksprings.enetlink.net
E-mail: rscmc@enetlink.net

Your Head or God's Head!

O' Lord our God, all this store that we have prepared to build thee a house for thine holy Name cometh of thine hand, and is all thine own (I Chronicles 29:16)

I will never forget the Winter of 2000. Our church had implemented the plans to build a 1100 seat worship center and we were beginning a Capital Stewardship Campaign. I was as nervous as could be an I was encouraging our members to pray and make a three year financial committment to the campaign. I also was praying along with my wife Barbara about what we should contribute. I finally reached an amount that was more than I had

---

Not Equal Gifts . . . But Equal Sacrifice

177

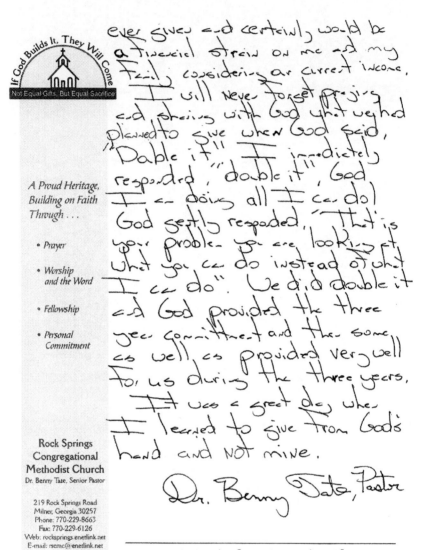

ever given and certainly would be a financial strain on me and my family considering our current income. I will never forget praying and sharing with God what we had planned to give when God said, "Double it." I immediately responded, "double it", God I am doing all I can do! God gently responded, "That is your problem you are looking at what you can do instead of what I can do". We did double it and God provided the three year commitment and then some as well as provided very well for us during the three years. It was a great day when I learned to give from God's hand and not mine.

Dr. Benny Tate, Pastor

If God Builds It, They Will Come

Not Equal Gifts, But Equal Sacrifice

A Proud Heritage, Building on Faith Through . . .

- *Prayer*

- *Worship and the Word*

- *Fellowship*

- *Personal Commitment*

Rock Springs Congregational Methodist Church
Dr. Benny Tate, Senior Pastor

219 Rock Springs Road
Milner, Georgia 30257
Phone: 770-229-8663
Fax: 770-229-6126
Web: rocksprings.enetlink.net
E-mail: rscmc@enetlink.net

Not Equal Gifts . . . But Equal Sacrifice

Your Hand Or God's Hand

"O Lord our God, all this store that we have prepared to build thee an house for thine holy name cometh of thine hand, and is all thine own." (I Chronicles 29:16)

I will never forget the winter of 2000. Our church had implemented the plans to build an 1,100 seat worship center and we were beginning a Capital Stewardship Campaign. I was as nervous as could be and I was encouraging our members to pray and make a three year financial commitment to the campaign. I also was praying along with my wife Barbara about what we should contribute. I finally reached an amount that was more than I had ever given and certainly would be a financial strain on me and my family considering our current income.

I will never forget praying and sharing with God what we had planned to give when God said, "Double it." I immediately responded, "Double it? I am doing all I can do." God gently responded, "That is your problem, you are looking at what you can do instead of what I can do." We did double it and God provided the three year commitment, and then some, as well as provided very well for us during the three years.

It was a great day when I learned to give from God's hand and not mine.

"The Christian Life is the only battle where victory is won through complete surrender." —Dr. Benny Tate

Dr. Benny Tate

"He learned to give from God's hand."

For our generation, Dr. Benny Tate represents the epitome of a pastor/motivator/evangelist surrendered totally to Christ and willing to teach others the principles he has been taught by the Holy Spirit. To know Dr. Tate is to be infected with contagious enthusiasm. He is enthusiastic about his relationship with Jesus Christ and about his relationship with his wife, Barbara, and daughter, Savannah Abigail. Married to Barbara for over 20 years, he calls her "the best pastor's wife." He tells his daughter that he would "rather be your dad than be President." He is excited, also, about the church he pastors and about motivating other people to reach their God-given potential.

Dr Tate received Jesus Christ as his personal Savior at 16 and at 17 started preaching at rescue missions, nursing homes, and jails.

While working as a janitor, Benny was challenged and motivated by a stepfather who believed in him. The unusual stepfather told him that he could be so much more, that "God had gifted him;" and that "every degree you complete, I will pay for!" Doubting his own ability and "scared to death" (because of his elementary and high school record), Benny obtained four degrees: Associate's, Bachelor's, Master's, and Doctor's—all paid for by his stepfather who believed in him!

A graduate of Andersonville Theological College and Covington Theological Seminary, now Dr. Tate pastors Rock Springs Congregational Methodist Church in Milner, Georgia.

The church has grown from thirty to an average attendance of over 1,000 under his leadership--the largest church in his denomination. As a person visits the church website, he understands the escalating excitement. The church body strives to reach people of every age, and they advertise, "If God Builds It, They Will Come." Much emphasis is placed on prayer. The church's radio ministry, *Apples of Gold*, is taken from Proverbs 25:11, "*A word fitly spoken is like apples of gold in pictures of silver.*" "Words can build us up or tear us down," as the stepfather taught Dr. Tate.

As a motivational speaker, Dr. Tate has spoken to corporations such as Delta Air Lines, ServiceMaster, Gold Kist, and Chick-fil-A, and we can understand his popularity with such remarks from Congressman Mac Collins, *"Benny is God's messenger to many who seem hard to reach. His message is always practical, easy to understand...with a mix of wit and humor."* John Lunsford (Georgia State Representative) calls him a *"real diamond—in a sea of imitation stones. His insight and intuitiveness are beyond his years. His personal tragedies (his wife Barbara was healed of seizures) and intense drive have molded a rare jewel for the Lord."*

The head football coach of Georgia Tech, Chan Gailey, calls Dr. Tate's book ***HAPPY WIFE, HAPPY LIFE*** "an excellent study on how God wants us to approach marriage as a husband and the leader of our family." Saxby Chambliss (U.S. Senator from Georgia) said "every married couple should read it, and for those about to marry, it should be required reading." Among many interesting points Dr. Tate makes is that we all need to take a lesson from "Mistresses Anonymous" ("mistresses are experts in the art of listening") and improve our listening skills! The book also includes excellent ideas (an understatement) on how to rear responsible, God-fearing children and grandchildren.

Perhaps a trademark of Dr. Tate's sermons, speeches, and books is the creative choice of words, startling statements, and the many humorous stories or illustrations. For example from one chapter in ***ONE MORE NIGHT WITH THE FROGS***, Dr. Tate jolts us by saying, "When a Christian marries a nonChristian mate, they are unequally yoked. The Christian immediately gets the devil for a father-in-law!" In another place, he says, "Do you know the largest Methodist, Presbyterian, and Assembly of God churches in our world are in Korea? Do you know the average Korean pastor prays for two hours a day? The average pastor in America spends eight to nine minutes a day in prayer."

"When we seek His face in personhood, He will give us His hand in provision."—Dr. Benny Tate

"Oh, that they had such a heart
in them
that they would fear Me
and always keep
all My commandments,
that it might be well with them
and their children forever!"
--Deuteronomy 5:29

Handwriting

convinces

others

about

your

identity!

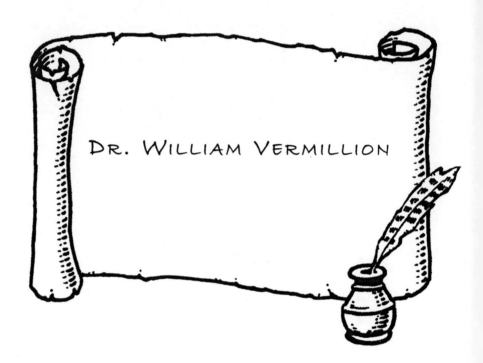

Dr. William Vermillion

THE OFFICE OF GENERAL SUPERINTENDENT

My greatest spiritual experience took place during a mission commitment in Russia from 2000-2003. During that time God caused me to confront issues of personal and national pride. In addition, He used this foreign culture to help me surrender my needs to be in control to Him. In this whole process I realized God was deepening His presence in my life. This process of growing maturity confirmed my need and desire to be more dependent on Him. I must continually be filled with the Holy Spirit. The result was an abounding love for God & for others as God was being more perfectly formed in me! PTL! To Him be all Glory!

William (Bill) Vermillion

My greatest spiritual experience took place during a mission commitment in Russia from 2000-2003. During that time God caused me to confront issues of personal and national pride. In addition, He used this foreign culture to help me surrender my need to be in control to Him. In this whole process I realized God was deepening His presence in my life. This process of growing maturity confirmed my need and desire to be more dependent on Him. I must continually be filled with the Holy Spirit. The result was an abounding love for God and for others as God was being more perfectly formed in me! PTL! To Him be all Glory!

William (Bill) Vermillion

DR. WILLIAM VERMILLION
"In The Lord's Army"

Since elected in 2002, Dr. William Vermillion has been the General Superintendent of the Evangelical Church, an organization whose spiritual roots go back to the ministry of Arminius, the seventeenth-century theologian, and to the Wesleyan revival.

A man whom God was preparing for Kingdom work from the time Dr. Vermillion was young, he says he at first spent many years in the educational system. He earned his B.A. from Washington State University in 1968, his M.A. in 1972, and the Ph.D in 1980 from the University of Washington. He taught as a professor at "various schools" and served as Administrative dean from 1985-1989 and again from 1996-1997. From 2000-2003 he served as Rector.

God continued to prepare him for His use when Vermillion served from 1969-1971 on active duty as a Captain in the U.S. Army Infantry Division, and then in the Reserves from 1971-1980. But Vermillion insists he has served "in the Lord's Army" actively since 1963 after he gave his life to Christ!

From 1973 until 2000, Dr. Vermillion served as associate pastor and then senior pastor of "various churches." He also did mission work in Indonesia, Honduras, and Bolivia, and "short term" in Russia.

Dr. Vermillion's life has been one of purpose, change, and much activity culminating in his office as General Superintendent. He is the author of "Pastoral Epistles" in the *Asbury Bible Commentary* and "Philippians" and "Philemon" found in the *Wesleyan Study Bible*. Born in Seattle, Washington, he and his wife now live in Minnesota.

"Knowing that I am not the one in control gives great encouragement. Knowing the One who is in control is everything."—Alexander Michael

"My son, keep your father's command, and do not forsake the law of your mother. Bind them continually upon your heart; tie them around your neck. When you roam, they will lead you; when you sleep, they will keep you; and when you awake, they will speak with you. For the commandment is a lamp and the law a light; reproofs of instruction are the way of life."
—Proverbs 6:20-23

GOD'S INTERCESSORS FOR THIS GENERATION

John Wesley said, *"God does nothing but by prayer, and everything with it."* E. M. Bounds re-iterated this idea when he said that God shapes the world by prayers. *"The more praying there is in the world the better the world will be, the mightier the forces against evil.... The prayers of God's saints are the capital stock of heaven by which God carries on His great work upon earth. God conditions the very life and prosperity of His cause on prayer."* (**The Necessity of Prayer**, Whitaker House, 1984). Ezekiel 22:30-31 states God *"sought for a man among them who would make a wall, and stand in the gap before Me on behalf of the land, that I should not destroy it;...."*

Biblical examples:

In 2 Chronicles 20:7, Abraham (probably the first intercessor mentioned in the Bible) is spoken of as "a friend of God." He became **intimate with God (a prerequisite for intercession)**. Because he **spent time with God,** Jehoshaphat, also, could ask God questions like, *"Shall not the judge of all the earth do right?" "O our God, will You not judge them? For we have no power against this great multitude that is coming against us; nor do we know what to do, but our eyes are upon You"* (2 Chronicles 20:12).

Another intercessor was Elijah. In 1 Kings 18:1 God told Elijah He was going to send rain to Israel. Even though it was God's will and timing to send the rain, **He still needed a human being to ask Him**. So it is recorded that Elijah asked seven times for the rain to begin before the answer came (1 Kings 18:41-45). James 5:17, 18 affirms that it really was Elijah's prayers that released the rain (*Elijah was a man with a nature like ours, and he prayed earnestly that it would not rain; and it did not rain on the land for three years and six months. And he prayed again, and the heaven gave rain, and the earth produced its fruit"*).

On another occasion, Daniel knew it was time for the nation of Israel to be restored from its captivity. Though it was **God's will and timing**, Daniel still **had to ask and to persist in prayer** until the angel broke through with the answer (Daniel 9:3; 10:13). A final example is found in Numbers 14:11,12 where Moses interceded. God made the announcement: *"I have pardoned, according to your (Moses') word."* The Judge of the universe pardoned a rebellious people because of the intercession and "words" of a human being! God is still doing the same today! *

Our Generation:
Though God calls intercessors for every generation, in recent months many have been more aware of this special group of people. Since September 11, 2001, when hi-jacked airplanes shattered the Twin Towers in Manhattan and part of the Pentagon near Washington, D.C., many Americans have met in intensified, concentrated effort to reach God for our generation. In most towns and communities small groups meet for prayer. We also have many prayer organizations thriving, such as **Prayer International Ministry**, the **League of Prayer** in Alabama, **Generals of Intercession** in Texas, the **Elijah House of Prayer** in Oregon, William Ford III's and Dutch Sheets' 2002 "**Kettle Tour**". Lou Engle has gathered more than one million people to pray and fast in 12-hour-long gatherings. The **Joshua Project** is a group of intercessors from sixty-two countries that come together to pray for revival at Harvard University. And the list goes on.

To reinforce and remind us of the purpose of this book project, I relate the story that was the catalyst for the 2002 "Kettle Tour" (**an intercessory prayer tour**) of Pastor Dutch Sheets and businessman, William Ford, III. The tour was an historic effort to pray over the Original Thirteen Colonies and New England asking for God's forgiveness for the atrocities and sins of the people and to intercede for each state.

"While ministering at my alma mater, Christ for the Nations' Institute, in Dallas, Texas, I [Dutch Sheets] was publicly praying that everything God had purposed for the Bible school would be accomplished. At that moment, I clearly heard the Lord respond to me, 'I need you to agree in prayer with the founder of the school, Gordon Lindsey.'

"My first thought was, 'I can't do that, God. He's been dead for 30 years.' The Lord clearly answered me again, 'But his prayers are

*The Beginner's Guide to Prayer, Dutch Sheets, Regal Books, p. 26.

not dead; they're still alive in heaven. *And there are things he asked Me for which I promised to give him—things I want to release into the school now. But I cannot do them until **this present generation** comes into agreement with his prayers'."*

Pastor Sheets says, *"God sees the generations as being much more connected than we do. He may promise a person something and do it through his or her grandchildren, for in His mind, doing it through a person's descendants is doing it for or through him or her."* *

As our ancestors prayed for our nation and for their descendents, we must continue re-enforcing their prayers for our nation and our children.

WE ARE NOT ALONE! Our generation is praying. We have concerned people who are "standing in the gap." One minister prayed, *"Not on my watch, Lord, not on my watch am I going to stand by and witness the spiraling downgrade of this Nation."* (Ten years ago, one researcher, Dr. David Barrett, speculated that the number of weekly prayer meetings being held worldwide may exceed 10 billion.)

Some Special Results of Prayers:

In her book ***Give Me 40 Days For Healing,*** Mrs. Freeda Bowers emphasizes the importance of asking God **how to pray in a given situation**. As she and an assistant went to the hospital to pray for a terminally ill friend, *God said, "Don't pray for the pain. Don't pray for the tumors to dissolve. Don't pray for her physicians to have wisdom. Don't pray for her immune system to activate."* The assistant said, *"Lord, we have nothing left to ask You. What do You need from us today for our friend?"* He said, *"Pray that her gifts and her calling live and not die, and I will command the temple that carries them to be whole!"*

From ***Manna From On High*** intercessor prayer group leader: *"A few weeks ago I received an urgent call for prayer. A young man in another state tried to commit suicide and his grandmother found him hanging from a rope. She cut him down thinking he was dead but realized there was still life within him. She put him in the car to rush him to an emergency room. On the way the frenzied boy awakened and realized his grandmother was trying to save Him, so he jumped*

*Dutch Sheets & William Ford, III, *History Makers,* Regal Books, 2004, pp. 13-14.

*from the car. She lost him in the rush of traffic. Immediately **I asked the Lord how I should pray** and I saw an image of a boy being driven to suicide by satan. The Lord let me know that **it was not the ordained time for this boy to die. I began to pray for divine intervention and claimed the right of this boy to live out his ordained time.** I knew God had intervened. Immediately thereafter, I saw a hate-filled sneering face and he said to me, "You just had to intervene, didn't you? I was so joyful that the words did not bother me. I knew God had taken over in this boy's life. I heard later that day that the boy had returned home and had asked his family to help him and to get help for his addiction. What I learned was that satan couldn't murder him before God's appointed time so he was driving him to suicide."*

A group of Christians were praying for a Muslim sheik who was confined to bed diagnosed with AIDS. The doctors told him there was no hope. One day Mohammed had a vision and Jesus told him to rise up, live, and serve Him. Mohammed became a Christian and was also healed. Since beginning his ministry as a Christian evangelist, he has led thousands of Muslims to Christ, and with his recent medical checkup he is free of AIDS.

Those interceding for family members should be encouraged by the story of Dick Eastman whose mother interceded for him. *"At the age of fourteen he had become involved in a life of rebellion and burglary. He and another young man had developed an effective scheme to prey upon unsuspecting patrons at the swimming pool, unobtrusively stealing purses or wallets while their owners were swimming."* One day his partner had set up a plan for another "heist," when suddenly Dick Eastman knew he could not take part. That night while his friend was committing a robbery (for which he was later sent to jail), Dick felt compelled to attend church. His mother's intercession had prevailed! Dick Eastman is now International President of Every Home for Christ. *

Persistence and desperation may be needed as we intercede for the need of someone. In fact, Bill Johnson says it is *"Absence of persistence and desperation {that} causes believers to miss God."* One intercessor said he prayed for a young girl in a coma for an hour or 2 a week for a year before she was healed. A pastor said he prayed an hour a day for a month before his wife was healed of an

*Edward K. Rowell, et.al. *1000 Quotes and Illustrations*, Baker Books, p. 349.

ovarian cyst. The story of George McCluskey's prayer life for his family is, likewise, an illustration of persistence. When McCluskey married and started a family, he decided to invest one hour a day in prayer because he wanted his children to follow Christ. Every day between 11 a.m. and noon, he prayed for the next three generations. Most of the descendants became ministers or married ministers. One descendant decided to pursue a career in psychology. That great grandson is Dr. James Dobson whose radio program is aired on thousands of stations each day! *

One final example of the effectiveness of intercessory prayer, and in this case, instruction to pray the word: A small group was praying for a couple who was facing bankruptcy. As they interceded, God spoke to the group saying, *"Pray My Word. Don't tell me how. Don't tell me when. Just return My Word to Me. I watch over My Word to perform it."* The group began praying scripture pertaining to God's plan for the couple's needs to be met, and they challenged the man and wife to pray the same way. (Deuteronomy 28: 8, 11— *"The Lord will command the blessing upon* [us] *in* [our] *barns and in all that* [we] *put* [our] *hand to, and He will bless [us] in the land which the Lord* [our] *God gives [us]. And the Lord will make* [us] *abound in prosperity,...."* Deuteronomy 28:13—*"And the Lord shall make* [us] *the head, and not the tail;"*; Psalm 25:12-14—*"Who is the man who fears the Lord*? [God] *will instruct* [us] *in the way* [we] *should choose...."*) Within months the couple was no longer facing bankruptcy and God was blessing them mightily.

In ***The Beginner's Guide to Intercession*** our generation was asked to do six things as we intercede for the lost: **

1) Pray that their spiritual eyes will be opened to truly see and understand the gospel (2 Corinthians 4:4 and Acts 26:18).
2) Ask that all deception be broken off the unbeliever (2 Corinthians 10:4-5).
3) Ask that the stronghold of pride in them will be torn down (2 Corinthians 4:4)—"blinded has in its meaning the concept of self-conceit or pride."

*Dick Eastman, *Love On Its Knees*, Chosen Books, 1989.
**Sheets, *Intercession*, pp. 63-73.

4) Pray that all of satan's strategies and schemes will fail.
5) Pray "that the Holy Spirit will hover around or envelop the unsaved person with His power and love" (Galatians 4:19).
6) Ask for workers—harvesters—to be sent to the unbeliever (Matthew 9:36-38).

Promise of Revival:

Abraham said to God regarding Sodom and Gomorra (Genesis 18:23-33) *"Will you sweep away the righteous with the wicked?* God replied, *"If I find fifty..., forty-five..., forty..., thirty..., twenty..., ten righteous people in the city of Sodom,* **I will spare the whole place for their sake."**

In spite of moral decay in our society, our generation is one of the most blessed and one that should be filled with tremendous hope. Though other countries have experienced revival, since 1906 historians say America has not experienced a major, all-encompassing revival. That situation is changing!

Many prayer warriors, ministers, and recent prophets have talked about the great revival that is coming to America. The late Dr. Fuchsia Pickett (ordained Methodist minister, dean and director of a college, conference speaker) related a vision God gave her where for two days she was taken into the heavenlies and shown that revival is coming first to five geographical areas within the United States and then spilling over into other places. God spoke to her about how He would prepare the church for His return and did this by using a hydroelectric plant as an analogy.

She transcribed her vision of the hydroelectric plant onto paper and later, while staying in Oregon, a friend took the transcript to the Pacific Power Company in Oregon and asked to see the head engineer. In a few days the president of the company wanted to see Dr. Pickett. When she entered his office, he wanted to know where she had obtained the information, for the paper *"was one of the most scientific"* he had ever read. *"Only a few master electricians know and understand this."*

At the time of her vision, God said, *"I am running the pipes now. And this time when I pull that great power switch and release all the rivers of my living Word in their fullness, no one will ever dam it up again. I will do a quick work; I am going to bring the revival that will result in the ingathering of the great harvest of souls."*

Dr. Pickett said after that experience as she ministered in various churches throughout the U.S., she would hear the sound of water (as in the hydroelectric plant vision) in those churches that God was going to visit with revival.* In the 1990's, Dr. Paul Yonggi Cho also prophesied that God was sending revival to America, especially to five different areas.

My intercessory prayer group:

The following section contains testimonies from six people in a prayer group similar to groups around the world. This group is special to me for they meet each week, and they cry out to God, *"Is there anything too difficult for the Lord?"* (Genesis 18:14). My prayer group consists of three widows, two housewives, a retired train engineer, an associate pastor, a retired real estate agent, an insurance agent, a land developer, one who works for the FBI, and one who owns and operates a major business (in a man's world!). They pray for our families, for our nation, for Iraq, for Israel, for the world. They are the salt of the earth!

"The great point is never to give up until the answer comes.... The great fault of the children of God is that they do not continue in prayer; they do not go on praying; they do not persevere. If they desire anything for God's glory, they should pray until they get it. Oh, how good, kind, gracious, and generous is the One with whom we have to do!" ---George Mueller

*Fuchsia Pickett, *The Next Move of God*, Creation House Publishers, 1994.

"Our fathers in Egypt did not
understand Your wonders;
they did not remember the multitude
of Your mercies,
but rebelled by the sea—the Red Sea.
Nevertheless
He saved them for His name's sake,
that He might make
His mighty power known....
They soon forgot His works;
they did not wait for His counsel,...
and He gave them their request,
but sent leanness into their soul....
They forgot God their Savior,
who had done great things in Egypt,
wondrous works in the land of Ham,
awesome things by the Red Sea.
Therefore He said that He would destroy them,
<u>had not Moses His chosen one</u>
<u>stood before Him in the breach</u>
to turn away His wrath,
lest he destroy them. "

-Psalm 106:7-23

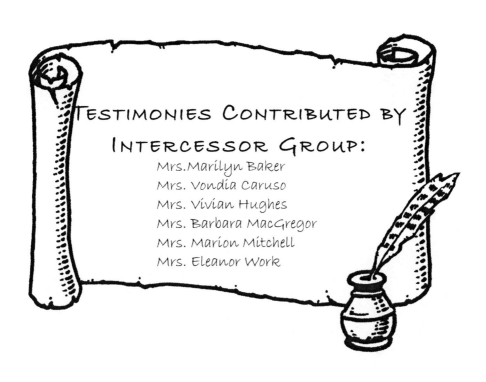

TESTIMONIES CONTRIBUTED BY

INTERCESSOR GROUP:

Mrs. Marilyn Baker

Mrs. Vondia Caruso

Mrs. Vivian Hughes

Mrs. Barbara MacGregor

Mrs. Marion Mitchell

Mrs. Eleanor Work

I was raised in a family that attended a small protestant church every Sunday, but I ceased going to any church after leaving home at age 18. At the age of 50, I gave my life to Jesus Christ and, thankfully, He led me to the right church and to the right people there to let me know God is very much alive. I was amazed to find He still performs miracles, heals, and casts out demons; all through His disciples. I also found out that He talks to us. While still a new Christian, I was provoking a Christian co-worker to read the Bible, because of her lack of knowledge of Scripture. She did start reading the New Testament every day on her lunch hour, but not without letting me know she was somewhat annoyed by my actions. I then started asking the Lord to forgive me for embarrassing her, when after the "umpteenth" time of asking, I heard "You did exactly what I wanted you to do." It took me by surprise, but then I realized who was speaking to me and thanked Him. I felt so loved!

Marilyn V. Baker

Mrs. Marilyn Baker

"Pure and undefiled religion before God and the Father is this: to visit orphans and widows in their trouble, and to keep oneself unspotted from the world."—James 1:27

A graduate of American Business College in Wichita, Kansas, Mrs. Marilyn Baker has spent most of her life working in the insurance field as an underwriter, marketing representative, manager, or agent. So successful was she as an insurance agent that, even after her official retirement in 1997, she was asked to return to work for a major company where she is still employed!

After her conversion at age fifty, she became employed at night and on weekends doing Kingdom Work. She attended Vision Christian University where she graduated in 1997 with a B.A. in Theological Studies. She has literally fulfilled the command in Isaiah 1:18, *"Learn to do good; seek justice, rebuke the oppressor; defend the fatherless; plead for the widow."* (Even before becoming a Christian, God put it within her heart to be a giver, as she contributed to the Rescue Mission and to Rev. Billy Graham.) She has worked in a jail/prison ministry and in the Women's Shelter of a Rescue Mission. Later, she began holding services at a retirement home. Faithful to God, to her church, and *"to one of the least of these My brethren,"* Mrs. Baker is blessed with good health, prosperity, joy, and a place in His Kingdom, because Jesus said, *"Assuredly, I say to you, inasmuch as you did it to one of these..., **you did it to Me.**"*-- (Matthew 25:40)!

November 7, 1971, I took my two children to a play given by the Youth Group at a Church. I was not a Christian even though I took them to Sunday School. At this event, when the Altar Call was being made, I had a powerful encounter with the Holy Spirit. I didn't know the scripture in Genesis 6:3 that says, "My Spirit shall not always strive with man", but I knew in my heart that was the last time He would deal with me. I had refused His promptings many times in my life. That night I gave up and said yes to God. I'm so thankful He invited me one more time.

Vondia Caruso

Mrs. Vondia Caruso

November 7, 1971, I took my two children to a play given by the Youth Group at a church. I was not a Christian even though I took them to Sunday School. At this event, when the altar call was being made, I had a powerful encounter with the Holy Spirit. I didn't know the scripture in Genesis 6:3 that says *"My Spirit shall not always strive with man,"* but I knew in my heart that was the last time He would deal with me. I had refused His promptings many times in my life. That night I gave up and said "yes" to God. I'm so thankful He invited me one more time.

For years Vondia and her late husband, Tony, had their own construction business, but now Vondia continues serving God doing volunteer work in a local hospital, working in her church, and meeting with a special prayer group. She has one son, Scott, and a daughter, Revonne.

Vondia is a leader. After attending Bible school, she became a licensed minister and has served as music minister, Bible teacher, vice president of a Women's Aglow chapter in one town, and for two years President of Women's Aglow in another area.

One of her greatest joys is writing inspirational poetry and songs. With permission we print one of her songs:

You're Somebody Special
Copyright © 1984 by Vondia Caruso

You're somebody special to Jesus;
You're somebody special to Him.
He created you to be, in His family tree
  A bright, shining jewel in His crown;
You're precious in His sight—
He loves you with all His might;
You're somebody special to Jesus.
  CHORUS: Praise His Name, O praise His Name;
                That you may display His virtuous ways;
                Praise His Name; just praise His Name;
                He formed you to show forth His praise.
You're somebody special to Jesus;
You're somebody special to Him.
You are in His chosen race
  A living stone of grace,
A royal child are you;
His own Blood has made you new;
You're somebody special to Jesus.

I have no one date that I can point to as to when I was "born again," but I had responded to a Billy Graham message on the radio numerous times in the months preceding my most memorable experience with God. As a child I grew up with a hunger to know what life was all about, and looking for answers, I turned to poetry, majoring in English literature in college. In the years preceding the "memorable experience" I'm referring to, I had developed a dependence on alcohol, and was seeking release from the trap I knew I had fallen into. Recently I had been invited to a Bible study in the home of an acquaintance, and the Bible teacher there had given me a book that she suggested I read. I could hardly wait to get home the next evening from my job as a real estate salesman to read her gift.

It was my habit when I arrived home to fix myself a coca cola with vodka. I fixed my usual drink and sat down at our coffee table. Opening the book I discovered a small New Testament — a gift to the lady herself, and inscribed from her own son-in-law. I felt indescribably unworthy, sitting there with my drink, and the thought, "I'll never ever be good enough to be a Christian," ran through my mind. It was then – slightly to my left and above me – there, in my own living room – was the presence that I knew was Jesus. I couldn't see Him, but I knew He was there. I called out something like, "Not now – I've got to get cleaned up first." But His presence didn't leave. It was as if low grade electricity was all about me,

and stayed with me for 3 or 4 hours. And as I read His
Word He made me so aware that His Word was
(& is) Truth, Power, & Reality, and that rightly
understood His Word held all my "answers". I've
never doubted that since. That date was June 30, 1972

Vivian Blodgit Hughes
Sept 2005
Bakersfull, California USA
Mother, Grandmother,
Great Grandmother
Daughter of the King
Elder First Presbyterian Church,
Bakersfull
Retired Realtor

"For God so loved the world that He gave His only
begotten Son, that whoever believes in Him should
not perish but have everlasting life."—John 3:16

MRS. VIVIAN HUGHES

I have no one date that I can point to as to when I was "born again," but I had responded to a Billy Graham message on the radio numerous times in the months preceding my most memorable experience with God. As a child I grew up with a hunger to know what life was all about, and looking for answers, I turned to poetry, majoring in English literature in college. In the years preceding the "memorable experience" I'm referring to, I had developed a dependence on alcohol, and was seeking release from the trap I knew I had fallen into. Recently I had been invited to a Bible study in the home of an acquaintance, and the Bible teacher there had given me a book that she suggested I read. I could hardly wait to get home the next evening from my job as a real estate salesman to read her gift.

It was my habit when I arrived home to fix myself a coco cola with vodka. I fixed my usual drink and sat down at our coffee table. Opening the book I discovered a small New Testament—a gift to the lady herself, and inscribed from her own son-in-law. I felt indescribably unworthy, sitting there with my drink, and the thought, "I'll never ever be good enough to be a Christian," ran through my mind. It was then—slightly to my left and above me—there, in my own living room—was the presence that I knew was Jesus. I couldn't see Him, but I knew He was there. I called out something like, "Not now—I've got to get cleaned up first." But His presence didn't leave. It was as if low-grade electricity was all about me, and stayed with me for 3 or 4 hours. And as I read His Word He made me so aware that His Word was (and is) Truth, Power, and Reality, and that rightly understood His Word held all my "answers." I've never doubted that since. That date was June 30, 1972.

Vivian Blodget Hughes
Sept 2005
Bakersfield, California USA
Mother, Grandmother,
   Great Grandmother
Daughter of the King
Elder First Presbyterian Church
Retired Realtor

I was in my high school years, early 60's, when my sister Alana and I were seeking & questioning the things of God. We were in our bedroom, a _detached_ converted garage. It was late into the night when we finally decided to go to sleep. We both said good night and turned away from each other. I recall it was warm as we only had a sheet for cover. Almost immediately after I closed my eyes I felt a sensation of the bed rising like a rocket into space. So much so I was afraid to open my eyes and look over the side of the bed. I turned over to my back and to look in the room. As I did Alana did the same. I told her of my sensation and she related the same to me. At this we both thought we'd perhaps been raptured or even died! It seems silly now but at the time it was very real.

As I began to look around the room I noticed some figure at the bottom of our bed. It was an outline of a person with great light behind it. I tried to see our desk and wall but this

figure blocked my view. I wasn't afraid of it but very curious. My sister was too afraid to look past the sheet around her face! I turned to her to tell her to look but when I looked back again the figure was gone. The next morning we told our mother who thought we were dreaming. But — later in the day a friend at School gave me a copy of "A Man Called Peter." A book Catherine Marshall wrote of her husband. In it she wrote of an almost identical figure at the foot of her bed. It was the Lord Himself who visited her to heal her of Tuberculosis!

I read this passage in study hall at school and almost couldn't believe what I was reading.

Over the years I've concluded that His appearing to my sister and I was to assure us that He was the "I Am" and we need not worry or question. Our faith took over from there!

Barbara McThesn

Mrs. Barbara MacGregor

I was in my high school years, early 60's, when my sister Alana and I were seeking and questioning the things of God. We were in our bedroom, a detached converted garage. It was late into the night when we finally decided to go to sleep. We both said good night and turned away from each other. I recall it was warm as we only had a sheet for cover. Almost immediately after I closed my eyes I felt a sensation of the bed rising like a rocket into space. So much so I was afraid to open my eyes and look over the side of the bed. I turned over on my back to look in the room. As I did, Alana did the same. I told her of my sensation and she related the same to me. At this we both thought we'd perhaps been raptured or even died! It seems silly now but at the time it was very real.

As I began to look around the room I noticed some figure at the bottom of our bed. It was an outline of a person with great light behind it. I tried to see our desk and wall but this figure blocked my view. I wasn't afraid of it but very curious. My sister was too afraid to look past the sheet around her face! I turned to her to tell her to look but when I looked back again the figure was gone. The next morning we told our mother who thought we were dreaming. But later in the day a friend at school gave me a copy of "A Man Called Peter," a book Catherine Marshall wrote of her husband. In it she wrote of an almost identical figure at the foot of her bed. It was the Lord Himself who visited her to heal her of tuberculosis!

I read this passage in study hall at school and almost couldn't believe what I was reading. Over the years I've concluded that His appearing to my sister and me was to assure us that He was the "I Am" and we need not worry or question. Our faith took over from there!

******

Barbara is faithful! Though young at heart and young in appearance, she says she has been actively involved in church work for over forty years ("since my teens"). She has an Associate Degree in Biblical studies and is an executive board member of her church.

In her spare time, she works full time (22 1/2 years) for the F.B.I., her "Bureau Career—not just a job."

Her one daughter, Carrie, and three grandchildren delight her life.

"And whatever things you ask in prayer, believing, you will receive."---Matthew 21:22

So far my most significant experience with God was when I finally dared to release my total self to Him - to dare to trust His plan for my life. It was like being let out of a smothering cave of my own making. I'm sure the demon of fear I allowed into my thought life smugly thought he had another victim.

For five years I had the tormenting fear that I was going insane. I didn't dare let my guard down for surely I would go out of control and end up in a snake pit for the hopelessly insane.

I'll never forget the day when I was lying on my bed exhausted from self absorbtion and self centeredness, I cried out to God. "O.K. God, I give up! You created me and You are sovereign. If it is your plan I end up locked up in an asylum - here I am!" I surrendered myself unreservedly to Him.

Of course the release was immediate. The freedom from the trap was so heavenly I'm sure Gods angels were rejoicing with me.

Marion Elizabeth Mitchell

MRS MARION MITCHELL

So far my most significant experience with God was when I finally dared to release my total self to Him--to dare to trust His plan for my life. It was like being let out of a smothering cave of my own making. I'm sure the demon of fear I allowed into my thought life smugly thought he had another victim.

For five years I had the tormenting fear that I was going insane. I didn't dare let my guard down for surely I would go out of control and end up in a snake pit for the hopelessly insane.

I'll never forget the day when I was lying on my bed exhausted from self- absorption and self-centeredness, I cried out to God. "O.K., God, I give up! You created me and You are sovereign. If it is your plan I end up locked up in an asylum, here I am!" I surrendered myself unreservedly to Him.

Of course the release was immediate. The freedom from the trap was so heavenly I'm sure God's angels were rejoicing with me.

My achievements are only those where Jesus and I were partners:

1. I am at peace with God.
2. I lived with one husband for 56 years.
3. I have two lovely daughters who know the Lord.
4. Two sons-in-law who serve the Lord.
5. Five grandchildren, one grandson-in-law and one granddaughter-in-law.
6. Five great-grandchildren who either know the Lord or who are being covered with prayer.
7. Many dear friends who are sisters in the Lord.
8. I manage my home and finances.
9. I have good health and freedom from debt.
10. I look forward to being in heaven with my Jesus and many loved ones.

*****

Marion Mitchell is dependable, adventurous (still swims everyday as weather permits), relies on God, and simply believes that God will do what He says He will do. Her late husband was involved in politics and they owned and operated a successful cattle ranch. Actively involved in her church and several prayer groups, Marion spends part of her time in California and part time relaxing at their home in Idaho.

"And His mercy is on those who fear Him from generation to generation."—Luke 1:50

"But the mercy of the Lord
is from everlasting to everlasting
on those who fear Him.
And His righteousness to children's
children to such as keep His
covenant, and to those
who remember His commandments
to do them."
-- Psalm 103:17

As a 14 year old teenager, God spoke to my heart and called me into His Kingdom. During the Sunday evening service in July of 1952, I gave my heart to the Lord. As I entered the auditorium, I sat on the back row with my heart yearning for that moment when I would "be saved". My mind could focus on nothing else. When the Pastor gave the invitation, I immediately responded and "floated" down the aisle, with no consciousness of my surroundings until I was approximately three steps from the Pastor, I was weeping deeply. I continued to weep (why, I did not understand) as I was given the right hand of Christian Fellowship. I immediately become aware of this "PRESENCE" in my heart. I could literally feel Jesus in my heart. He was so real to me. The awareness of HIS presence went with me as I left the church on that July night. That moment and time become the most memorable a life changing encounter of my life. I had truly become a new creature in Christ.

Eleanor Work

214

Mrs. Eleanor Work

As a 14-year-old teenager, God spoke to my heart and called me into His Kingdom. During the Sunday evening service in July of 1952, I gave my heart to the Lord. As I entered the auditorium, I sat on the back row with my heart yearning for that moment when I would "be saved." My mind could focus on nothing else. When the Pastor gave the invitation, I immediately responded and "floated" down the aisle, with no consciousness of my surroundings until I was approximately three steps from the Pastor; I was weeping deeply. I continued to weep (why, I did not understand) as I was given the right hand of Christian Fellowship. I immediately became aware of this "PRESENCE" in my heart. I could literally feel Jesus in my heart. He was so real to me. The awareness of HIS presence went with me as I left the church on that July night. That moment and time became the most memorable life-changing encounter of my life. I had truly become a new creature in Christ.

Eleanor Work communes with God, cares about people, and is a peace-maker. She is a member of her church "praise team" and for fifty years has been singing in duets, trios, or solos! She has been married for 47 years to one man, her high school sweetheart, Robert. Besides God and her church family, "family" is uppermost in her mind: *"I am the mother of two beautiful, Godly daughters (my greatest achievement), Teresa Moore and Juli Jennison. I have 3 wonderful grandsons, Josh, Jonathan and Jeremy and 2 beautiful granddaughters, Hannah and Maddie."*

"And as for Me, this is My covenant with them --those who turn from transgressions--says the Lord, 'My Spirit which is upon you, and My words which I have put in your mouth, shall not depart from your mouth, nor from the mouth of your offspring, nor from the mouth of your offspring's offspring,' says the Lord, from now and forever."
-- Isaiah 59:21

"The righteous shall flourish like a palm tree.
He shall grow like a cedar in Lebanon.
Those who are planted in the house of the Lord shall flourish in the courts of our God.
They shall still bear fruit in old age; they shall be fresh and flourishing, to declare that
the Lord is upright; He is my rock, and there is no unrighteousness in Him."
--Psalm 92:12-15

What does the comparison mean?

"The palm grows not in the depths of the forest nor in a fertile loam, but in the desert. Its verdure often springs apparently from the scorching dust. 'It is a friendly lighthouse, guiding the traveler to the spot where water is to be found.' The tree is remarkable for its beauty, its erect aspiring growth, its leafy canopy, its waving plumes, the emblem of praise in all ages. Its very foliage is the symbol of joy and exultation. It never fades, and the dust never settles upon it. It was, therefore, twisted into the booths of the feasts of tabernacles, was borne aloft by the multitude that accompanied the Messiah to Jerusalem, and it is represented as in the hands of the redeemed in Heaven. For usefulness, the tree is unrivalled. Gibbon says that the natives of Syria speak of 360 uses to which the palm is applied. Its shade refreshes the traveler. Its fruit restores his strength. When his soul fails for thirst, it announces water. Its stones are ground for his camels. Its leaves are made into couches, its boughs into fences and walls, and its fibers into ropes or rigging. Its best fruit, moreover, is borne in old age, the finest dates being often gathered when the tree has reached a hundred years. It sends, too, from the same root a large number of suckers, which in time, form a forest by their growth. What an emblem of the righteous in the desert of a guilty world!"

--Joseph Angus (1816-1902)
English clergyman

*"For the Word of God is **living** and **powerful**, and **sharper** than any two-edged sword, piercing even to the division of soul and spirit, and of joints and marrow, and is a discerner of the thoughts and intents of the heart."*--Hebrews 4:12

Is it not a strange phenomenon? Words written on a piece of paper and placed in a book are "living and powerful, and sharper than a two-edged sword." The *MESSAGE* Bible states, *"**His** powerful Word is sharp as a surgeon's scalpel, cutting through everything, whether doubt or defense, laying us open to listen and obey. Nothing and no one is impervious to God's Word. We can't get away from it—no matter what."*

And is it not strange John 17:23 records Jesus saying that His Father loves us as much as He does Jesus? ….*"and that the world may know that You have sent Me, and have loved them as You have loved Me."* In the natural world, many parents with more than one child usually have a favorite (though admission would bring anathema!). In the spiritual realm, God has millions and millions of children; yet, He loves each one as much as He loves His Son, Jesus the Christ!

Is it not strange, also, that in the natural world a love-letter is usually shared between two people, and, for anyone "eavesdropping" (letter-reading), the letter has no special importance. In the Spiritual realm, God shares His love-letter (The Holy Scripture) with millions and millions of people and to each one who reads it, the Word seems to speak only to him or her. That is the power of God's Word!

Soren Kierkegaard said, "When you read God's word, you must constantly be saying to yourself, 'It is talking to me, and about me'." George Mueller (British missionary who founded many orphanages) maintained, "The vigor of our spiritual life will be in exact proportion to the place held by the Bible in our life and thoughts. I solemnly state this from the experience of fifty-four years. The first three years after conversion I neglected the Word of God. Since I began to search it diligently, the blessing has been wonderful. I have read the Bible through one hundred times, and always with increasing delight. Each time it seems like a new book to me." Martin Luther also affirmed, "The Bible is alive, it speaks to me; it has feet, it runs after me, it has hands, it lays hold of me."

For Mrs. Samuel Hynd, the wife of a third generation missionary to Africa, God's Word became life for her in the following account:

MRS. PHYLLIS HYND

One of the Outstanding Experiences in my life when God has spoken to me, was when He called me to be a Missionary Nurse. He has been faithful to speak to me through the scriptures. It seems I have an enlighted understanding as I read the scriptures. The words seem to be written for me — Romans 12:1 — "to offer your bodies as a living sacrifice, holy and pleasing to God" — I ask God, who me?? As I tried to argue with God, He seemed to say, "Listen to me." I knew then God would lead each step. As my life began to unfold in Nurses training, College, University and on to Midwifery training in Scotland I was aware of His presence. This presence was my strength, courage and determination to do "His will". I spent 36 years in Swaziland. His strength sustained me. Whether it was in the delivery room, as a New life was born, or through the long hours of the night, caring for a Critically ill patient. His presence was abiding!

15 months Scotland — Midwifery training
36 years in Swaziland — Missionary Nurse
28 years married to Dr. Samuel W. Hynd
   He was the physician for the King
   and Royal family. I assisted him.

PHYLLIS HYND

One of the outstanding experiences in my life when God has spoken to me, was when He called me to be a missionary nurse. He has been faithful to speak to me through the Scriptures. It seems I have an enlightened understanding as I read the Scriptures. The words seem to be written for me—Romans 12:1—"*to offer your bodies as a living sacrifice, holy and pleasing to God*"--. I asked God, who me? As I tried to argue with God, He seemed to say, "*Listen to Me.*" I knew then God would lead each step. As my life began to unfold in nurses training, college, university and on to midwifery training in Scotland, I was aware of His presence. This presence was my strength, courage, and determination to do "His will". I spent 36 years in Swaziland. His strength sustained me whether it was in the delivery room, as a new life was born, or through the long hours of the night caring for a critically ill patient. His presence was abiding!

15 months Scotland—midwifery training
36 years in Swaziland—missionary nurse
28 years married to Dr. Samuel W. Hynd. He was the physician for the King and Royal family. I assisted him.

"Come to Me, all you who labor and are heavy laden,
and I will give you rest. Take My yoke upon you
and learn from Me,
for I am gentle and lowly in heart,
and you will find rest for your souls,
for My yoke is easy and My burden is light."
—Matthew 11:28-30

Mrs. Samuel (Phyllis) Hynd
"Living in The Present Is Like Threading A Needle"

At the age of 16, God spoke to Phyllis Hynd from Isaiah 6:8-9 to go into full time Christian service. *("Also I heard the voice of the Lord, saying: 'Whom shall I send, and who will go for us?' Then I said, 'Here am I! Send me.'")* At an early age, Phyllis had established the habit of meeting with God an hour (usually 5 a.m.) in Bible reading and prayer before attending classes or going to work.

Taking her nurses training in the U.S., Mrs. Hynd became a registered nurse and then spent fifteen months in Glasgow, Scotland, specializing in midwifery training. From there she went to Swaziland, South Africa, working with the Swazi people, learning the SiSwati language and their customs. (It is very impolite to hand anything to one of their people with your left hand; you shake hands with the right hand with the left hand on your right wrist.) Mrs. Hynd learned to love the Swazi people.

After thirteen years, she met and married Dr. Samuel Hynd, a third generation medical missionary to South Africa. For twenty-six years she served along side Dr. Samuel Hynd at the Manzini Medical Centre.

When Dr. Hynd became Minister of Health for Swaziland and the personal physician to King Sobhuza II and Mswati III, Phyllis said the ministry to the royal families *"became very precious. Seeing God work in their lives as we delivered new members of their families has been exciting in spite of long hours required for their medical care."*

With changing events, they witnessed the devastation of the aids virus that destroyed lives, families, and communities. Patients swarmed in from all areas of Swaziland to the Manzini Medical Centre, and the heavy load on the staff took its toll. Like Paul of Bible days who suffered affliction, rejection, and persecution, the

Hynds suffered, also. Bouts with malaria, deafness, and depression wreaked havoc on Mrs. Hynd.

Phyllis, impressed by a quote from Walker Percy, says she has learned that to live in the past and future is easy. To live in the present is like threading a needle. In a newsletter to a friend she wrote that she takes comfort from a quote in Philip Yancey's book, *Reaching for the Invisible God*, who reminds us that the Apostle Paul mentions three Christian virtues: faith, hope, and love (1 Corinthians 13). *"Love involves caring about people most of us would prefer not to care about. Hope gives us the power to look beyond circumstances that otherwise appear hopeless. Faith always means believing in what cannot be proven, committing to that of which we can never be sure."*

Mrs. Hynd has reached out in recent days in new faith (still rising early to read God's Word) and she knows *"God holds the future in His hands, and my hope is in our great God!"*

"It is the Spirit that quickens; the flesh profits nothing; the words that I speak unto you, they are spirit, and they are life."—John 6:63

"Then they shall know that I am the Lord God."

--Ezekiel 28:22,23,24,26
Ezekiel 29: 16,21
Ezekiel 30:8,19,25,26
Ezekiel 32:15
Ezekiel 33:29
Ezekiel 34:27,30
Ezekiel 35:4,9,12,15
Ezekiel 36:11,23,38
Ezekiel 37:6,13
Ezekiel 38:23
Ezekiel 39:6,7,22,28

One Doggie, One Kitty, "Fishies," And The Prayer Of A Child

For forty-seven years, one has walked in our midst who was raised from the dead, so I was elated early one Saturday morning when the caller said, "Hello. This is Betty Malz. I have just come home from the hospital after having open-heart surgery, and I want to take part in your book project. Am I too late?"

After receiving Mrs. Malz' testimony, I expected her "lasting impression about God" to relate something of the twenty-nine minutes in 1959 when she was declared clinically dead. Instead of telling about her natural father (as he stood by her lifeless body) saying, "Jesus," (thus catapulting Betty from heaven to earth again) Betty Malz told of another miracle, probably just as great a miracle, having to do with a child's prayer and God mercifully and tenderly fulfilling the request. I like to think God is telling us something significant: that building faith, especially in a child, and having the faith of a little child, is as important as being raised from the dead.

"Then they brought little children to Him, that He might touch them; but the disciples rebuked those who brought them. But when Jesus saw it, He was greatly displeased and said to them: **'Let the little children come to Me and do not forbid them; for of such is the kingdom of God. Assuredly, I say to you, whoever does not receive the kingdom of God as a little child will by no means enter it'.** *And He took them up in His arms, laid His hands on them, and blessed them."*
--Mark 10:13-16

"Faith is the invisible energy that produces visible results as we act on the belief that God is our good Father and that He wants to lead us into His good will."-- Betty Malz

225

Testimony

convinces

others

about

God's

reality!

MRS. BETTY MALZ

Betty Malz
P.O. Box 364
Crystal Beach, FL 34681
(813) 786-3249
727

North Terre
Haute, Indiana

"You can't Take It With You!"

My husband and I took great pride. After
saving for ten years we had built the
long, ranch style house we dreamed
of. It was 4 feet longer than any in
our family, adored by relatives.

My husband had to work until 9:00
p.m. Our six year old daughter, Brenda
and I, watched "Lassie" (T.V. series) and
munched warm home made pop corn.
Suddenly the porch light went out and
the television began cracking and popping.
The picture went blurry and divided.
There was a rumbling overhead like
ten freight trains.

We rushed to the bedroom, against
an inside wall and prayed.
Little Brenda prayed, "Oh God don't let
Snukey, my little doggie, blow away,
don't let "Disco" kitty die, keep my
fishies safe!"

The puppy came immediately
and crawled safely under her body.
The unannounced tornado took 36
houses in our subdivision. We only
had one wall left standing in ours.

228

Betty Malz
P.O. Box 564
Crystal Beach, FL 34681
(813) 786-4249
127

The following morning the "Grit"
Newspaper photographer showed up.
They photographed one of our books
in the mud "GONE WITH THE WIND".
our car was crushed, but kitty
was safe underneath. A 2×4 had
blown into the aquarium, but
not one gold fish was harmed.

after the highway was opened up
and the Red Cross arrived, my husband was able to find us in the
basement of the one undamaged
house nearby.

At this point we decided to
quit ~~things~~ fretting about, and
collecting THINGS and INVEST
IN PEOPLE. (The only thing you can take
with you is people)

Betty Malz

Betty Malz has written 11 books
that are translated into 14
different Languages.

You Can't Take It With You!

P.O. Box 564
Crystal Beach, FL 34681

My husband and I took great pride, after saving for ten years, we had built the long, ranch style house we dreamed of. It was 4 feet longer than any in our family, owned by relatives.

My husband had to work until 9:00 p.m. Our six-year-old daughter, Brenda, and I watched "Lassie" (T.V. series) and munched warm home-made pop corn. Suddenly the porch light went out and the television began cracking and popping. The picture went blurry and wild. There was a rumbling overhead like ten freight trains.

We rushed to the bedroom, against an inside wall and prayed. Little Brenda prayed, "Oh God, don't let Smokey, my little doggie, blow away. Don't let "Disco" kitty die, keep my fishies safe!" The puppy came immediately and crawled safely under her body.

The unannounced tornado took 36 houses in our subdivision. We only had one wall left standing in ours.

The following morning the "Grit" Newspaper photographers showed up. They photographed one of our books in the mud "GONE WITH THE WIND". Our car was crushed, but kitty was safe underneath. A 2 x 4 had blown into the aquarium, but not one gold fish was harmed.

After the highway was opened up and the Red Cross arrived, my husband was able to find us in the basement of the one unharmed house nearby.

At this point we decided to quit fretting about, and collecting THINGS and INVEST IN PEOPLE. (The only thing you can take with you is people.)

Betty Malz

Betty Malz has written 11 books that are translated into 14 different languages.

Mrs. Betty Malz

A Survivor Who Invests in People

*"Back in Union Hospital, my dad was so heartbroken he stood by my bed and sobbed 'Jesus'. He moaned that name to comfort himself, but in that one-word prayer, he wished that I had not died. I never wanted to leave that glorious place [heaven], but hearing him utter that name changed my mind. Returning to my body—not much of a body since I weighed only 68 pounds upon my return—I experienced resurrection. I saw the **Word** written in light and coming to me. It was John 11:25: **'I am the resurrection, and the life; he that believeth in me, though he were dead, yet shall he live'.** I touched the Word and sat up, very much alive."*

These are the words of Mrs. Betty Malz, a twentieth and twenty-first century follower of Jesus Christ, a go-getter, time bomb for our Redeemer. She is the author of eleven books, three of which were on the *Times* Best Seller List. *My Glimpse of Eternity* sold over 2 million copies in eighteen languages. She also is the lady who (at twenty-nine years), after her appendix ruptured and the organs became gangrenous, lay in a coma for 44 days in Terre Haute Union Hospital. Then she died and spent twenty-nine minutes in heaven. *My Glimpse of Eternity* is Mrs. Malz' description of her experiences in heaven and how, through her father's grief and prayer, she returned to her body.

Mrs. Malz described the heaven-encounter transition as serene and peaceful. She realized she was not alone, that a masculine-looking figure in a robe (an angel) walked at her side, and she felt they were no strangers, that they had always known each other. She said she felt she had everything she had ever wanted to have and she was everything she had ever intended to be. She described a twelve-foot high gate made of a solid sheet of translucent pearl. As the two moved along, she saw a yellow light that appeared dazzling, and she became conscious of another person. **"Suddenly I knew that the light was Jesus, the person was Jesus."** Several times she continued to hear the voice of her earthly father saying 'Jesus'; even though she would like to remain in heaven, her **thoughts** communicated with the angel and she was taken back to Terre Haute, to the hospital, and to the room where she saw a figure on the bed with a sheet pulled over it (her own body).

While Betty was in a coma, a nurse placed a *No Visitor* sign on her door and allowed no noise in the room. "Yet during that time," Betty said she "heard celestial strains of music around me, in the room and overhead." Apparently she thanked the nurses "for playing that awesome music for me." The nurses told her family, "She keeps hearing music, though we have allowed no noise in her room." In heaven, she heard melodious music in many-part harmony, and she heard many different languages, yet she understood them all! (After forty-plus years, Mrs. Malz' heaven encounter continues to be discussed and "rationalized" by various people and groups on the Internet.)

At ten years of age, Betty started playing the accordion that led to a lifetime interest in music. She was often called on to play the organ or piano in her church. In her books about heaven, she tells of the importance of music both in this life and in heaven. During her heaven-encounter she heard Jack Holcomb singing. Later she called Holcomb's residence (hoping to tell Jack she had heard his music in heaven) only to be told by Mr. Holcomb's widow that Jack passed away 2 years previously!

From the time she was eight-years-old, Betty dreamed of being a writer—one who "would write books showing the way to Jesus, salvation, and the unseen world." **God has granted her heart's desire!** The recorder is partial to *Morning Jam Sessions,* dedicated to her daughters April Dawn and Brenda. One wonders how a writer can discover so much interesting information to inspire other people with a one-page devotion for each day of the year! Mrs. Malz observes life, finds delight and a message in every pebble and encounter, and she is not afraid to reveal her inmost thoughts that provide a mixture of "laughter and spiritual medicine." She often writes ten to fourteen hours a day, keeping notes under her bed, in her bathroom, in her purse!

In one entry she exhorts the reader about knowing who our enemy is when someone hurts us. *"Don't waste energy ranting and scheming against the people who cause you pain. Aim your ammunition at the right target—the devil. Go after him!"* In another encounter she relates how in an animal orphanage, a cat slapped at her and she knew immediately, by first impression, that she and the cat belonged to each other! First impressions are vitally important and *"we never get a second chance to make a first—or a last—impression."*

One of her most popular books, *Making Your Husband Feel Loved,* is a collection of "secrets" from twenty-five Christian women who share their ideas on how to make a marriage more vibrant, fresh, and alive. The "secrets" are from such women as Joyce Meyer, Lisa Bevere, Cathy Lechner, Brenda Timberlake, Lindsay Roberts, and Pamela Smith.

Many of her books, such as *Heaven, Touching the Unseen World, and Angels Watching Over Me,* are exhortations about how the reader can prepare for and what to expect in another world! In *Supernatural Living* and *Prayers That Are Answered,* Mrs. Malz tells of her experiences with God and some of the things she has learned. One prayer warrior commented that even though a person thinks they know a lot about prayer, Mrs. Malz' books will teach you more. *Simplicity: Kingdom Living Through the Eyes of a Child* makes us stop and examine our priorities. Most of us say that love and family are our top priorities, but do we really live as though they are? One thing Mrs. Malz learned as she was returning from her heaven-encounter: *"I was suddenly aware of God's love for all his churches. It was a sudden bit of knowledge, as if I were being told this on the inside by the Holy Spirit. At that moment I loved all his churches too; and as my prejudices dissolved, I loved all his people."*

Betty was reared in a minister's home, and after her first husband's early death from a heart attack, she married Carl, a missionary and college director. She has had two daughters and three stepchildren. She now lives in Florida.

Mrs. Malz is a survivor. In fact, her publisher recently told her (after she had spent five days in intensive care from an automobile accident) that her next book should be *This Cat Has Nine Lives!* Mrs. Malz has experienced unusual heartaches (death of a husband, a daughter, open heart surgery), but she insists that a sense of humor (She jokes about her 5'12" height!) and the ability to laugh sustain her. Thus, she writes and continues to speak in churches, at retreats, conferences, and on television.

In a television interview with her daughter (who was born four years after Mrs. Malz' trip to heaven), the host introduced the daughter by saying, "and here is the daughter who was born four years after her mother's death!" Betty laughs and says the audience was stunned and shocked.

Mrs. Malz modestly says she doesn't have a very interesting biography! However, she stresses one thing that life and her husband, Carl, have taught her. While Carl was in Europe, he met and became a friend of Mother Teresa (who died at 97). As she worked with "undesirable" people and at one point had just rescued an elderly man by using a spoon to dig maggots out of a head wound and then pouring hydrogen peroxide in the opening, Carl asked her, "How do you do this?" Mother Teresa replied, "Carl, God insures His tools and His equipment. Invest in people." Mrs. Malz makes that her aim! During a telephone conversation, she reminded me to tell the people: One thing is important and that is to INVEST IN PEOPLE!

"I am the resurrection, and the life; he that believeth in me, though he were dead, yet shall he live."-- John 11:25

"Where were you when
I laid the foundations of the earth?
Tell Me, if you have understanding.
Who determined its measurements?
Surely you know!
Or who stretched the line upon it?
To what were its foundations fastened?
Or who laid its cornerstone, when
the morning stars sang together,
and all the sons of God
shouted for joy?"
--Job 38:4-7

"Light" Reflectors Or Market-place Christians

"There was a man sent from God, whose name was John. The same came for a witness, to bear witness of the Light, that all men through him might believe. He was not that Light, but was sent to bear witness of that Light." --John 1:6-8

During our generation a new phrase became commonplace: "marketplace Christians." Though Christians have always ministered in the "marketplace," a movement among some leaders began that reached outside the church to preach the good news of Salvation.

This marketplace ministry emphasized that God, indeed, is interested in prospering the Christian businessman or businesswoman. A "calling" to "G*o into all the world and preach the gospel...*" could be other than a calling to become (after attending a seminary or Bible college) a pastor or minister. Many believed that great revival would come to America through God using young people and through those in the work place. Various groups encouraged young people to obtain training to become entrepreneurs, to enter politics, to become educators, to become medical doctors—in short, to become successful Christians who could witness in the work place for Christ.

Parallel to the movement in the 1980's of many parents home-schooling their children, a similarity in the church world surfaced (to the concern or dismay of some Church leaders) with the emergence of "home churches" (not cell groups"). In some large cities, home churches met in homes or businesses. They were led, not by a seminary graduate, but often by a company CEO. Emphasis was placed on worship, Bible study, and witnessing to those in the work place. To meet the needs of such groups, institutes and seminars to train leaders for the "church revolution" became popular.

The following "special encounters with God" of three marketplace Christians testify to the love and mercy of our Heavenly Father as He leads people to succeed in the area to which He calls them.

Ms. Lesa Hashim

Narrow Your Vision, My Child

One of my most significant encounters with God was a vision I had on a Sunday afternoon when I was 23-years old. I had just crawled into bed for a late-afternoon nap and as I closed my eyes I was instantaneously transported to the streets of New York City. There were tall, gray buildings on each side of me & people everywhere! My ears filled with sound; I could hear sirens wailing in the distance, horns honking, the click-clock of dress shoes on pavement, and the chattering of people engrossed in conversations. The city was alive; its energy palpable. I surveyed my surroundings in complete awe! "This city is amazing! Our world is amazing!" Excitement rose in my chest and I found myself yearning to explore, explore, and explore! I wanted to see it all! I walked slowly down the street, looking in every direction in an attempt to process all the stimuli around me. After awhile, I looked left and saw a really long & narrow alleyway leading to a dim light. My curiosity compelled me to investigate so I turned & made my way slowly down the alley. As I walked, the sounds of the city

of my life for I know that the love &
happiness I feel today are only the
beginning of the eternal rewards that
await me! Praise be to God!

Colossians 3:1-3 Since then, you have been
raised with Christ, set your hearts on
things above, where Christ is seated at the
right hand of God. Set your minds on things
above, not on earthly things. For you died, and
your life is now hidden with Christ in God.

Resa M. Haslin

Narrow Your Vision, My Child

One of my most significant encounters with God was a vision I had on a Sunday afternoon when I was 23 years old. I had just crawled into bed for a late-afternoon nap and as I closed my eyes I was instantaneously transported to the streets of New York City. There were tall, gray buildings on each side of me and people everywhere!

My ears filled with sound; I could hear sirens wailing in the distance, horns honking, the click-clock of dress shoes on pavement, and the chattering of people engrossed in conversations. The city was alive, its energy palpable. I surveyed my surroundings in complete awe! "This city is amazing! Our world is amazing!" Excitement rose in my chest and I found myself yearning to explore, explore, and explore! I wanted to see it all!

I walked slowly down the street, looking in every direction in an attempt to process all the stimuli around me. After awhile, I looked left and saw a really long and narrow alleyway leading to a dim light. My curiosity compelled me to investigate so I turned and made my way slowly down the alley. As I walked, the sounds of the city behind me began to wane and the walls on either side of me seemed to rise even further into the sky!

Soon, I was walking in almost complete darkness, except for the dim light shining directly in front of me. The passageway became narrow, so narrow that I had to walk one foot in front of the other and push my hands out against the walls for balance.

FEAR overtook me and in the midst of my panic, I began to pray. "Lord, please help me! Please, please help me. I'm scared to death! I don't know where I am and I don't know where I'm going. I don't know how to keep going!" A voice within me spoke and encouraged me to "Continue On." Somehow, I did.

When I finally reached the end of the tunnel, the light was so blinding that I held my hand up to shield my eyes. I walked out of the darkness onto a terrace overlooking miles and miles of picturesque parkland with beautiful rolling hills and lush vegetation. Instantly, my fear left me and I was filled with an ineffable feeling, unlike any I have ever felt. It was as if God and His infinite blessings were all around me! I was overwhelmed with <u>LOVE</u>, <u>JOY</u>, <u>COMFORT</u>, and <u>PEACE</u> all at once! What a wondrous feeling! I rejoiced and praised God. God is love. God is joy. God is everlasting peace and happiness. I lingered on the terrace for a while, bathing in the light of the Lord and feeling HIS love envelop me. It was THE most profound experience of my life.

After the vision ended, I thought for some time about its meaning. **I realized that I was so mesmerized by the world and its temporary rewards that I was unable to focus on the deeper things that God has hidden, those things that are revealed only to those who daily seek His face and presence.** It was clear that God would have to narrow my vision in order for me to experience the unlimited joy that results from my TRUE calling.

Through my vision, God showed me, in a very real way, that His will for my life is infinitely better and more fulfilling than the path that I would choose for myself. **He certainly got my attention and from that moment on, I no longer put value in the things of this world, but dedicated by life entirely to the Lord for His use.** It was the best decision of my life for I know that the love and happiness I feel today are only the beginning of the eternal rewards that await me! Praise be to God!

Colossians 3:1-3: *"Since, then, you have been raised with Christ, set your hearts on things above, where Christ is seated at the right hand of God. Set your minds on things above, not on earthly things. For you died, and your life is now hidden with Christ in God."*

Lesa M. Hashim

LESA HASHIM

"And it shall come to pass afterward that I will pour out My Spirit on all flesh; your sons and your daughters shall prophesy, your old men shall dream dreams, your young men [and women] shall see visions."—Joel 2:28

Various prophecies have been given saying it is the youth whom God will use to bring revival to our nation! Lesa Hashim represents not the X-generation, but an explosion of youth presenting Jesus Christ **to our generation**. As much as is humanly possible, "All's right with the world" when young "market place" Christians pillar our generation.

At eleven years of age, Lesa received Christ as her Savior; however, a great change occurred a few years later that she tells about in her "encounter." She realized God had a special love for the person she really was and that He had a plan for her life.

Lesa is a typical but untypical twenty-first century young person. She enjoys her friends and family, but when they are not around, she enjoys time alone reading books that teach something new or that are of an historical nature. Friends say she is an inspiration to them because "When she sets her mind to something, she doesn't ever let anyone or anything stop her. She is never idle but thinking, learning, and absorbing life." A friend wrote an e-mail describing Lesa. He said, "When Lesa listens her ears hear the words from your mouth, but her eyes pierce deep into you to uncover what you are really saying. She can see that you're wringing your hands and saying everything is fine with your lips when she knows that it isn't. When she speaks you know she's speaking to you from the heart. She puts weight behind every word like your great-grandfather would"!

Lesa Hashim does not emphasize her formal training, saying that the most important training is that which has been going on for years with her Heavenly Father. "He is grooming me for something." She completed her B.S. degree in Political Science from UCLA and during her junior year in college did a Congressional Internship with Congressman William Thomas in Washington, D.C. After college she moved to NYC for two years, working for a media company. She also spent one year in a "study-abroad program for Shakespeare and Cultural Arts" in Florence, Italy, where she became a fan of English poetry, specifically Shakespeare and Tennyson.

Certainly a market place Christian young person, Lesa currently is studying for the Real Estate Broker's Exam while working for a land development company. She also is responsible for developing and maintaining an Internet site for a Christian ministry. Her greatest achievement or reward has come from relationships that are fulfilling with God, family, and friends (hoping to add 'husband and children' to that list, she says, 'and sooner than later'!).

Her only regret in life is that "sugar" is not included in our recommended daily allowances!

When God spoke to a man or woman in Scripture, He required obedience ("Noah, build a boat"; "Peter, go tell the Gentiles the truth about My plan of salvation"). When He speaks today, He requires the same response. **God spoke to Lesa and she tells how she obeyed and how her life changed.**

"My son [or daughter], if you accept
My words and store up
My commands within you, turning your ear to
wisdom and applying your heart to
understanding, and if you call out for insight
and cry aloud for understanding, and if you look
for it as for silver and search for it as for hidden
treasure, then you will understand the fear of the
Lord and find the knowledge of God,
for the Lord gives wisdom,
and from His mouth
come knowledge and understanding.
He holds victory in store for the upright;
He is a shield to those whose walk is blameless,
for He guards the course of the just
and protects the way of His faithful ones.
Then you will understand what is right and just and
fair—every good path.
For wisdom will enter your heart, and knowledge
will be pleasant to your soul.
Discretion will protect you,
and understanding will guard you."
--Proverbs 2:1-12

THE ULTIMATE FLIGHT

"When a parent or grandparent dies, a piece of your history is gone. When your spouse dies, a piece of your present is gone. When your child dies, you lose a piece of your future."

The picture on the reverse page is Mike Mueller flying, taken by one of his buddies. The sunburst is known as "the flyer's cross." Pilots often look for this sign to determine their landing possibilities.

MRS. NAOMI MUELLER

When our son Mike, a United States Naval Academy graduate, and his instructor were killed May 20, 1987 in a FA-18 crash, Psalm 18:30 became my verse, "As for God, His way is perfect."

In the valleys of life, we learn more of God. Even God doesn't make mountains without a valley in between. When days look the most bleak, God comes through! When the winds of adversity blow and your faith is tested, you find God's promises sure and steadfast.

A few months after May 20, 1987, my vision was further expanded and God added Psalm 18:32, "He girdeth me with strength and maketh my way perfect." Strength for each day and "making my way perfect?" How could I ask for more!

Naomi Mueller

When our son Mike, a United States Naval Academy graduate and his instructor were killed May 20, 1987 in a FA-18 crash, Psalm 18:30 became my verse: "As for God, His way is perfect."

In the valleys of life, we learn more of God. Even God doesn't make mountains without a valley in between. When days look the most bleak, God comes through! When the winds of adversity blow and your faith is tested, you find God's promises sure and steadfast.

A few months after May 20, 1987, my vision was further expanded and God added Psalm 18:32, "He girdeth me with strength and **maketh my way perfect**." Strength for each day and "making my way perfect?" How could I ask for more!"

Naomi Mueller

Mrs. Naomi Mueller

Naomi Mueller and her husband Don Mueller represent the "market place" Christians of our generation. Naomi (who grew up in a minister's home) received her Bachelors of Music Education and Masters of Music Education from the University of Tulsa, Oklahoma. From 1966-1985, she was Professor of Piano at Oklahoma Wesleyan University, Bartlesville, Oklahoma. While uncommonly active in their church and community, Naomi and Don owned and operated Mueller Realtors and Developer in Bartlesville. Recently, in honor of the Mueller family, the Mueller Sports Center was dedicated at Oklahoma Wesleyan University, Bartlesville.

Since their retirement in 2000, they live in Colorado but remain actively engaged in their church, in traveling, in serving on various advisory boards, and in doing missionary work (especially in building churches) in different parts of the world. In addition, Naomi plays the piano for her church and gives "some" music lessons, while Don "builds a house each year." With two daughters and five grandchildren who continue to be the joy of their lives, they are kept very busy. This year in honor of their son Mike's 20th anniversary graduation from USNA, Naomi and Don attended the Marine Corp Marathon held in Washington, D.C. Naomi said, "This touched us deeply, reminding us of the brevity of life and the importance of living for Jesus and others."

To understand and appreciate the perseverance of a couple in such heart-rending trials after their son's death is to thrill at the way God meets us and brings us through our deepest valleys. Surely as a testimony for future generations, God is pleased with the faithfulness of Naomi and Don.

Martha Chamberlain, friend and writer, followed in the footsteps of Naomi and Don while researching the mysterious circumstances (and "cover-up by the government") surrounding their son Mike's disappearance/crash. She produced ***The Ultimate Flight,*** a book with foreword written by George Beverly Shea.

To read the book is to be amazed at the mysterious events and to see why Mike (whose remains are at Arlington National Cemetery) was of a nobler class. At one point in the book Mike says of his mother and father, "I think you're the perfect parents...."

Referring to Naomi, the writer said, "*She can quote more scripture than a Southern Baptist evangelist. But it's not the quoting that gets you; it's the way she's lived it (seldom crying, always encouraging others to have faith) during these gut-wrenching months*" when she did not know where her son was or what had happened to him. (The plane went down May 20, 1987, and was found in June, 1988.) The greatest lesson we can learn, as Naomi did, is that God's ways are perfect (yes, we know that!) but surprise of all surprises (if we obey and permit Him), **He makes <u>our</u> way perfect, also**!

"As for God, His way is perfect;
the word of the Lord is proven;
He is a shield to all who trust in Him.
For who is God,
except the Lord?
And who is a rock, except our God?
It is God who arms me with strength,
and makes my way perfect."
--Ps. 18:30-32

DR. MARY RUTH SWOPE

Dr. Mary Ruth Swope

Apostle To The Market Place
February 19, 2004

Dear Reader,

In my 68 years as a believer in Jesus Christ of Nazareth, God has been good to give me hundreds of spiritual experiences (visions, dreams, impressions, rhema words) in which I have sensed His presence, felt His power, received His personal guidance and obtained His blessing.

My most significant experience, however, is not hard to identify. On February 7 & 8, 1977 I heard the audible voice of God speak to me three times. Here are the words.

"I am going to use you again in nutrition".

"I want you to ask American Christians to deny themselves unneeded calories, save the money the calories would have cost and give it to Great Commission projects and programs, in these last days."

The next day the same voice audibly spoke saying, "Put that in the form of an experiment. See if you can get Christians to do that."

In four weeks, 25 Christians denied themselves nearly one million calories, lost an aggregate of 87 pounds and saved $599.96.

To my knowledge that was my greatest success to date. I keep on trying, even in other nations, but not many Christians are into denying self – especially food.

Dr. Mary Ruth Swope

1819 Cr. 1596 ~ Avinger, TX 75630 ~ Phone: (903) 562-1777 ~ Fax: (903) 562-1750 ~ E-Mail: mrswope@aol.com

254

Dr. Mary Ruth Swope

www.maryruthswope.com

In my 68 years as a believer in Jesus Christ of Nazareth, God has been good to give me hundreds of spiritual experiences (visions, dreams, impressions, rhema words) in which I have sensed His presence, felt His power, received His personal guidance and obtained His blessing.

My most significant experience, however, is not hard to identify. On February 7 & 8, 1977 I heard the audible voice of God speak to me three times. Here are the words.

"I am going to use you again in nutrition."

"I want you to ask American Christians to deny themselves unneeded calories, save the money the calories would have cost and give it to Great Commission projects and programs, in these last days."

The next day the same voice audibly spoke saying, *"Put that in the form of an experiment. See if you can get Christians to do that."*

In four weeks, 25 Christians denied themselves nearly one million calories, lost an aggregate of 87 pounds and saved $599.96.

To my knowledge that was my greatest success to date. I keep on trying, even in other nations, but not many Christians are into denying self—especially food.

"Apostle To The Market Place"

B.S.—Winthrop College, Rock Hill, S. C.
M.S. in Foods and Nutrition from the Woman's College of the
University of
North Carolina, Greensboro
Ed.D.—Teacher's College, Columbia University, New York City
Seven years high school in home economics programs
Served as nutritionist with the Ohio Health Department
Foods and Nutrition faculty at Purdue University
Head of Foods and Nutrition at the University of Nevada
Head of Home Economics at Queens College, Charlotte, N. C.
Dean of the School of Home Economics, Eastern Illinois
University, Charleston, Illinois, 18 years
*From 1960-1980 conducted nine projects and wrote thirty-seven
professional journal publications.*

The recorder and readers of our generation view Dr. Swope with admiration for the education, the achievements, and the recognition that this market place Christian has attained. For that reason, I listed her achievements first. She has held lectures, seminars, and retreats; made television and radio appearances including the Christian Broadcasting Network's *700 Club*; Trinity Broadcasting Network's *Joy; It's A New Day; Today, the Bible, & You; the Southwest Radio Church; LeSea Broadcasting,* and others.

Besides her leadership as a nutrition expert at several colleges and universities, Dr. Swope has had at least two missions or callings to our generation. The author of eight books, she has labored to bring America to an awareness of sound nutrition. Her book, *Lifelong Health,* is a "scripturally-oriented nutrition sourcebook" that should be the delight of every mother, for it "contains sound dietary guidelines, spiritual nourishment, and delicious recipes." She and her son-in-law, a medical doctor, researched the material for her book *Green Leaves of Barley: A Food With Real Power.* Sick or well, people would be in better health if Dr. Swope's research were taken seriously. (Green Barley works!)

Born in Chillicothe, Ohio, Dr. Swope says that during her first year at college she "repented of her sins and invited Jesus Christ to be her Savior." When she had problems she did as most Americans have been taught: talk to a pastor or a doctor or a friend or a psychologist. "It is seldom suggested that we personally seek God's advice." **Perhaps the most interesting part of Dr. Swope's life is what happened to her later in her life.**

Despite degrees and achievements, Dr. Swope readily admits that real success came to her and her late husband after she attended a seminar on prayer. Until this event she said her prayers had been prayers basically asking God to bless **her** plans. Attending a Change the World School of Prayer Seminar, she learned how "to be still" and let God speak to her. Though reared in church and though she did all the right things, she had never realized that she could know God personally and have Him talk to her. As many Christians do, she said she "had been praying to a vague God way out there in the heavens somewhere." Further, as she looked back on her life, the only expectation in prayer to God "**had been to encourage Him**" to help her achieve the goals she wanted to attain! When tragedies occurred in her life she became desperate to know God personally and it was then her life changed (--from *Hearing God's Voice*)!

For the benefit of future generations and because many people desire to know God as Dr. Swope discovered Him, I list some of the ideas she learned about prayer:

--Prayer is communication with God.

--We should "spend 51 percent of our prayer time in listening prayer by asking God a question and then waiting in His presence for an answer."

--A literal prayer closet is a good place to retreat for hearing from God.

--Listening "is an art that must be cultivated and developed. It is God's business to speak to us; it is our business to be still and listen." (…"*He (the Holy Spirit) will tell you where to go and what to do.*"--Galatians 5:16. *"Everyone that is of the truth hears My voice."*-- John 18:37)

--Stillness is a prerequisite; "anxiety and strain will evoke silence from God."

--We must have an expectant attitude—God hears and will speak to us.

--from *Hearing God's Voice*

Being scientifically gifted and yet a person of "simple faith," Dr. Swope decided to try this teaching as an experiment. She reminds us "the only way I know to find time for waiting upon God is through the lonely valley of self-denial and personal discipline." When she first began listening prayer, many months passed before she began hearing from God. Her book reveals the blessings that listening prayer and time spent in her prayer closet brought to her life. She learned to seek God before making any decision. Through Scripture, personal words, and dreams, God's guidance helped her "make important decisions and fulfill His plan" for her life! It is a must read book.

In asking God why it had taken so long for her to discover the truth about listening prayer (having been a Christian for some forty years), she said she realized that her heart had not been seeking after God. Instead, she "was seeking after success and glory in the world system." Since establishing a prayer closet, Dr. Swope finds prayer a joy and "spiritual growth accelerated" more than all the previous years of her walk as a Christian.

As God began to communicate to her in thrilling ways, Dr. Swope was able to minister to various students on campus. She began receiving messages and words of knowledge for direction for herself, her family, and for the body of believers to encourage them. After eighteen years, God spoke to her to resign her job as Dean of the School of Home Economics at Eastern Illinois University, and she and her late husband, Don, took early retirement to begin the ministry of Nutrition With A Mission. God gave them the name for the business, gave them contacts, and led them to the entire world with the Biblical message about nutrition. Literally, overnight their lives were changed requiring them to open an office, employ people, and fill orders (after a TV program on Chelation therapy). Eventually they opened Swope Enterprises.

> Books or booklets Dr. Swope has written and tapes produced are the following:
> *The New Health Model*--tape
> *Newer Concepts In Nutrition*--tape
> *Are You Tired of Being Sick and Tired* (*Now Lifelong Health*)
> *Nutrition for Christians*

Green Leaves of Barley: A Food With Real Power
The Spiritual Roots of Barley
Green Leaves of Barley: Inspiring Secrets of Nature's
    Miracle Rejuvenator
The Roots and Fruits of Fasting
Some Gold Nuggets in Nutrition (booklet)
It's Not Too Late—video
Using Nutrition As Medicine—video
Hearing God's Voice
Listening Prayer
Bless Your Children Everyday

An energetic and vivacious woman, Dr. Swope continues to direct the family business. Her son, Stephen, and daughter, Susan, are equally involved in educating Christians about Biblical principles of nutrition. Their vision is that of *"helping believers and unbelievers shape up both spiritually and physically."* Dr. Swope writes and holds seminars, and she is well past fifty! In fact, the recorder received notes of encouragement at various times during the formation of the project and Dr. Swope would include a note such as, "I am 85 1/2 years old! When can we expect a copy of your work?"

"The most fruitful and satisfying time of my life has been those years since I learned to hear God's voice. Receiving and following God's guidance has led me down exciting paths that my feet would otherwise have never touched. Again and again His wisdom and counsel have made this business of daily living the super-satisfying, abundant life Jesus promised."
           --Dr. Mary Ruth Swope

"...publish [proclaim] with the voice of thanksgiving, and tell of all Your wondrous works." —Psalm 26:7

"So you shall keep His statutes
and His commandments
which I am giving you today,
that it may go well with you
and with your children after you,
and that you may live long
on the land which the
Lord your God is giving you for all time."
--Deuteronomy 4:40

"The thief does not come except to steal, and to kill, and to destroy. I have come that they may have life, and that they may have it more abundantly."—John 10:10

George Macdonald once stated that no words can express how much the world owes to sorrow. "Most of the Epistles were written in a prison. The greatest thoughts of the greatest thinkers have all passed through fire. The greatest poets have 'learned in suffering what they taught in song.' In bonds Bunyan lived the allegory that he afterwards put into words, and we may thank Bedford Jail for the *'Pilgrim's Progress.'* Take comfort! When God is about to make pre-eminent use of a man or woman, He puts him in the fire."

*"He **restores** my soul;*
He leads me in the paths of righteousness
For His name's sake."
--Psalm 23:3

*"So I will **restore** to you the years*
that the swarming locust has eaten,...
I am the Lord your God, and there is no other.
My people shall never be put to shame."
--Joel 2:25-27

*"And the Lord **restored** Job's losses when he prayed for his friends.*
Indeed the Lord gave Job twice as much as he had before."
--Job 42:10

The next testimony is a story of God's mercy in granting a desire to begin anew:

261

Handwriting

convinces

others

about

your

identity!

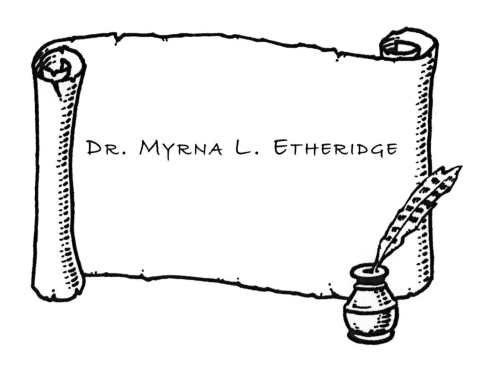

DR. MYRNA L. ETHERIDGE

During the most difficult time of my life – while I lived in Puerto Rico – God did a very special work in my life that implanted peace.

A student was in satan worship. Prayers entreated God, "if you created satan and are more powerful than him – Please, show me how to demonstrate your power for good." A book "How to be Baptised in the Holy Spirit" was given to me by a "unique" Baptist friend. It was read, obeyed and at the time to confess known sin and ask for the Baptism with the Holy Spirit – I did it. My heart was totally sincere.

The bedroom wall opened in a vision of Heaven. My ears heard only singing in tongues which became softer then louder accompanied by ray of color from the Holy City that was a distance from me. My mind questioned about the other side of the river – instantly I was on the other side – then back – then convicted about doing an experiment with God! He instructed me, must do.

The peace was wonderful. My request (thought) was to stay. My marriage was ended. My sons were dead. I knew I was to return and do what God had planned for me – whatever that was. It is now 33 years and nine books and much ministry later. God alone is LORD! Myrna J. Aldridge

MYRNA L. ETHERIDGE

During the most difficult time of my life—while I lived in Puerto Rico—God did a very special work in my life that implanted peace.

A student was in satan worship. Prayers entreated God, "If you created satan and are more powerful than he is, please, show me how to demonstrate Your power for good." A book How To Be Baptized In The Holy Spirit was given to me by a "unique" Baptist friend. It was read, obeyed and at the time to confess known sin and ask for the Baptism with the Holy Spirit—I did it. My heart was totally sincere.

The bedroom wall opened in a vision of Heaven. My ears heard only singing in tongues which became softer, then louder, accompanied by rays of color from the Holy City that was a distance from me. My mind questioned about the other side of the river— instantly I was on the other side—then back—then convicted about doing an experiment with God! He instructed me, mind to mind.

The peace was wonderful. My request (thought) was to stay. My marriage was ended. My sons were dead. I knew I was to return and do what God had planned for me, whatever that was. It is now thirty-three years, nine books, and much ministry later. God, Jesus is LORD!

Myrna L. Etheridge

www.gmeministries.org
P. O. Box 564
Sikeston, MO 63801

DR. MYRNA L. ETHERIDGE
"God really does let people start over!"

Sometimes our problems seem small compared to those who have gone through deep despair. Dr. Myrna Etheridge's life is a story of courage, of courage even when there seemed to be no hope. Because of a desperate hour, when everything and everyone had forsaken her, Myrna experienced a better understanding of Scripture, of faith, of the fear of God, and of the awesome love of God—none of which she would have without a season of despair. **For our generation and for future generations** Dr. Etheridge shows us what God says about diseases brought on by generational curses, and she also tells future generations that **God "really does let people start over!"**

How does a person cope with despair? What does a mother do after death takes her only two sons, and stress--experienced during the fiery trial--brings divorce to the two parents? What does one do when life seems not worth living? To Myrna Etheridge, the thought of suicide seemed a way out. However, to meet hospital and doctor expenses, she turned to her job and became fiercely involved in taking more courses, teaching in many schools and colleges, achieving more degrees, and becoming very successful through presenting various scientific papers. In 1967, Myrna obtained a grant from the National Science Foundation to study at the University of Puerto Rico. She is listed in several (nine!) Who's Who books in America and Europe. She has a BSE and MSE in biology from Arkansas State University. (Later she was awarded two Doctor of Divinity degrees and earned a Ph.D. in Systematic Theology.) An accomplished musician, she performed professionally as vocalist and organist, but **refused to allow herself to think, ever, about herself**. Amid the success, however, her personal life was in shambles and death seemed to haunt her thoughts. She remained alone in Puerto Rico.

Finally, while teaching USAFE classes for the University of Puerto Rico, Myrna met a friend who told her about a Comforter. She began to seek God intensely and after being baptized with the power sent from God (*"When the Comforter is come...He shall baptize you with the Holy Spirit and with fire,...."*--Luke 3:16), Myrna began to grow spiritually.

God began to answer Myrna's prayer "Please, God, give me the chance to start over." **She learned to praise and thank God continuously. Prayer and joy grew within her, and God began to teach her from the Scripture about healing for genetic diseases and about curses that are passed from one generation to another.**

Dr. Etheridge turned her heart and time to praying for others, and during this time of despair she became aware that **"God really does let people start over!"** As she prayed for people, she grew to love them as the Father had loved her. **Agape**, the God-kind of love, became her motivational driving force. (She has been known--as she later crisscrossed the United States ministering to other people—to spend most of the night in a hotel room praying for the city and its residents.) In addition, she began, over a period of time, to receive healing from anemia, from symptoms of cystic fibrosis in her own body, from dyslexia, and from allergies.

Born in St. Louis, Missouri, Myrna "came to Jesus at nine years of age in the church her family attended for two generations." At nineteen years of age she married and had two sons, both of whom had cystic fibrosis, a chemically malfunctioning, genetically inherited disease. Keith the youngest lived for 8 months, and Kirk, the first-born lived 3½ years. According to medical doctors, one out of every twenty from northern European ancestry has this genetic trait, and "one in four-hundred Caucasian couples would have the same genetic potential for cystic fibrosis children." Myrna and her husband both had inherited the genetic trait for the disease.

Cystic fibrosis meant her sons could not always play with other children;

> meant taking digestive enzymes with each meal and antibiotics;
> meant many trips to the hospital;
> meant sleeping in a "mist tent;
> meant "valuing my child by the day, never allowing thoughts about when he would be grown."

In her book *Momma, What's It Like to Die?* Myrna said, *"On the outside I laughed and smiled at my children.... I seldom cried. The pain of seeing [them] each day was my quiet, guilty burden. If only I didn't have this strange genetic gift to bequeath death to my children instead of life.... Knowing one is the source for a child's disease was a pain of the soul for which I had neither understanding nor relief. It was a fact. I didn't know any way to change it, so I had to accept it."*

Often Myrna would pray, *"Please work a miracle, if it is Your will and Your plan. If not, help me to be strong. Help me not to fear. Help me to live each day to its fullest. Please, Lord, help me walk through the valley. God, grant us the grace to accept your will."* She believed God was in control but she "didn't understand anything about getting what faith [she] had to grow."

"This hereditary disease, her own severe disability in learning, and the pain of divorce caused Myrna to begin the search for WHY?" God used her natural talents and training in science and biology to do intensive Bible research on the causes of illness. She documented what God taught her, and she recorded the message in **Momma, What's It Like to Die?** and **Fearing No Evil**. As a result of what she learned from her study, she has prayed for and witnessed deliverance for other families and she brings the message of hope to our generation: **family curses can be broken and "God really does let people start over!"**

At 12 years of age Myrna went forward in a Billy Graham Crusade and felt God's call to "Go wherever I tell you." After her family was gone, she continued to teach in public schools and colleges for eighteen years because she **"did not understand that a woman could teach the Bible."** In 1978 she resigned to begin writing about her experiences and to let others know about Scriptural teaching on genetic diseases.

Dr. Etheridge says that a "genetic disease doesn't have to be a life-long death sentence." Salvation, deliverance, and healing come in the complete atonement Jesus suffered for us! The death of Jesus on the cross, the stripes He took for us are for healing of our bodies. He "paid the debt for freedom for believers from diseases visited upon children of disobedient, unrepentant forebearers to their great, great grandchildren"—three generations according to Deuteronomy 23, 27, and 28. The blood, shed by Jesus "covers the believer's sins so that he is the righteousness of Jesus Christ, Y'shua!"

Dr. Etheridge tells extensively of her experience in "unlocking genetic diseases," and how others have been delivered by following

268

what she learned. Very briefly we mention a four-step process she recommends for obtaining deliverance from inherited diseases:

1. "Become obedient, broken and humble before the Lord. Pray and seek the Healer, not the healing. Fast, confess your sins and the sins of your fathers'. Confess what sins you know about. Become able to die to yourself and to be alive to God's leading. (Matthew 6:33, Isaiah 58:6, Nehemiah 9:2, Galatians 2:20)

2. "Confess that Jesus has paid the price for your freedom from genetic diseases on the cross. Praise God aloud that you are free as are your children through the tenth generation from genetic diseases. (Daniel 9:3-11, Nehemiah 8:18-9:3)

3. "Ask for a creative, restorative or recreation miracle. Pray and let God lead you as to what to ask for. (John 14:13-18, I John 5:14-15)

4. "Expect a gradual reversal of symptoms if the change is not immediate. Praise God daily for Jesus' perfect sacrifice. Because of it, you, your household and those you pray for are strengthened and continue to be made whole by the power of Jesus' name and the work of the Holy Spirit. Praise God for what He continues to do."

"...Weeping may endure for a night, but joy comes in the morning."
—Psalm 30:5

Dr. Myrna Etheridge "just happened" to go to the Post Office one morning in January 1979. Boaz called a similar situation "hands full on purpose;" Sarah laughed when an "angel" appeared to her; **Myrna calls her visit "the loving mercy of God."** That morning in the Post Office in Sikeston, Missouri, Myrna met a pastor friend, "a Baptist preacher of long years and a casual acquaintance" whose wife of 33 years had died two months previously. June 30, 1979, Dr. Grady and Dr. Myrna were married. For both of them "God let them start over!"

They now combine their teaching-anointing to minister together (or separately). They have appeared on TBN "Joy," Total Christian

TV, and other Christian TV and radio programs throughout the U.S. and Canada. One of their great joys is to find a "preacher boy" about the age Kirk or Keith would have been and nurture his education. Myrna continues to write (eight books last count!) and they travel holding Bible seminars, retreats, ministering to local church bodies, or to individuals desiring "to start over"!

"Surely He has borne our griefs
and carried our sorrows;
yet we esteemed Him stricken, smitten by
God, and afflicted.
But He was wounded for our
transgressions;
He was bruised for our iniquities;
the chastisement for our peace was upon
Him,
and by His stripes we are healed."

--Isaiah 53:4-5

AN OVERCOMER

"What things were gain to me, those I counted loss for Christ...I count all things but loss for the excellency of the knowledge of Christ Jesus my Lord; for whom I've suffered the loss of all things, and do count them but dung, that I may win Christ. --Philippians 3:7-8

Abigail Van Buren illustrated the power of God working in a person's life to overcome obstacles when she wrote:

"--Cripple him, and you have a Sir Walter Scott.

--Lock him in a prison cell, and you have a John Bunyan.

--Bury him in the snows of Valley Forge, and you have a GeorgeWashington.

--Make him play second fiddle in an obscure South American orchestra, and you have a Toscanini.

--Deny her the ability to see, hear, and speak, and you have a Helen Keller."

To this list we would add:

--Blight her early childhood with words like "retarded,"

--Attack her with the fear of flying,

--Take her husband, son, and loved ones,

--Strike her with various illnesses, **and you have an overcomer such as Dr. Mary S. Relfe.**

The following story of Dr. Relfe is the story of absolute trust and faith in Jesus Christ, of absolute abandonment to Him.

One person said, "I've never read a greater testimony to the power of God operating in a life and making a person an overcomer."

"The people that do know their God shall be strong, and do exploits."—Daniel 11:32

DR. MARY S. RELFE

League of Prayer

P.O. Box 680310
Prattville, AL 36068

I declare the vision is certain. After much meditation, solitude, reflections and study, I asked the LORD to grant me understanding in the visions of God... I submit unto you some prudent assessments which I believe were given me by the Holy Spirit. God came to me, attended a League of Prayer Board Meeting, and gave me permission to share with others that:

HE is Founder and Chief Executive Officer of League of Prayer.

He just appointed this earthly mortal to oversee it.

Mary D. Relf

HE CAME TO ME

April 5, 2004, the Holy Father came to me. With 200 Heads of State and millions converging on Rome to honor the deceased pope, God came to me! I've had a number of visions, three of Jesus, but never of the "Holy Father!"

In the vision God came to me in a long corridor which led to a spacious room. No introduction was needed. I knew Him, loved Him, was pleasantly comfortable in His presence. Imagine after all these years enjoying the hospitality of the Host of the universe!

In retrospect, one of the most remarkable impressions of this vision was the absence of dread and the unbounded comfort of His presence. It was like meeting a dear friend, devoid of any element of surprise, or any question with respect to His unnatural appearance. His height was normal, but His garment was "King Size." The large white robe was draped over His head and flowed around Him to the floor similar to a wedding gown. No feature of His body was visible. He was alone, that is no visible entourage accompanied Him. When He came to me, it seemed there was business to conduct and we immediately began walking toward a large Meeting Room. I noticed our stride was in synch! Walking with the King of Kings!

Just prior to entering the Room, I looked over at Him and asked: "How are these people going to look upon you for no man can see your face and live?" (Neither was I seeing His face.) Together we walked in the Room where a Head Table was prepared up front for two. We sat down at the table and for the first time I observed His garment had changed from plain white to glistening as if studded with myriad of tiny diamonds. Sitting beside me His robe had a huge circumference. Only a dozen or so people were present in the first row. Then, I surmised it was a Board Meeting. Since I only conduct meetings for League of Prayer, I perceive God was our Special Guest at a League of Prayer Board Meeting.

The Members expressed no more surprise than I had at His presence. Interchange between the Members and the Head Table commenced. As soon as a question was posed, the answer was immediately known by all. It seemed I chaired the Meeting, but it appeared He actually conducted it. Let me just say it was an unexampled business session, one in which I neither had nor took any notes. When the Meeting was adjourned, He vanished from sight and I awakened.

This rendezvous with His Majesty held sway over my body for hours. Upon rising, I was wiped out and my heart skipped beats....Reflecting or writing on it invokes an unusual anointing, which in part, I've walked in for some weeks.

Prayer is a dialogue, never a monologue. I said: "Why me, Lord?" Why would the high and lofty one who inhabits eternity desire to company with me? He said: "Daughter..."I dwell in the high and holy place, with him also that is of a contrite and humble spirit, to revive the spirit of the humble and the heart of the contrite ones." (Isaiah 57:15). Did I not say that in the last days I would pour out my Spirit upon all flesh—sons, daughters, young, old, servants and handmaidens shall prophesy, see visions and dream dreams? Acts: 2:17-18.

DR. MARY S. RELFE

A Life of Heartaches, Miracles, and Blessings

Always wanting to bring Glory to God, Dr. Relfe is one who is hesitant about sharing many of her thoughts and experiences. She said, *"It is my prayer that sharing this (about a miraculous healing of her body) will cause you to seize upon this resurrection power, and refuse to let Him go until He blesses you."* The recorder's desire is that the life of Dr. Mary Relfe will inspire future generations to do great things for God knowing (as Mary Relfe knows) that *"**The people that do know their God shall be strong and do exploits"** --Daniel 11:32.

How can one woman accomplish so much? Dr. Mary S. Relfe represents one in our generation who lost all, yet chose to follow Jesus Christ. A hurricane for God, Mary says, *"My life has been spent striving to hold God closely without being terrified of Him."*

Well educated, highly intelligent and articulate, an adventurer, a defender of the needy and helpless, a prayer warrior, an author of several books, including **When Your Money Fails**, and **Cure of All Ills** (A history of revivals), Dr. Relfe's beginnings were very humble. Born into a poor family, the middle of six children, she was believed to be "retarded" because of her quietness. However, Mary took God's challenge to become ambitious for God and to bring glory to Him. A foundation of her life and ministry is the adamant belief that *"The people that do know their God shall be strong, and do exploits."*

Once an average student in high school, she became "captivated" and inspired by Proverbs 1:7, *"The fear of the Lord is the beginning (the principal part) of knowledge."* This understanding led her to make straight A's the remainder of her high school years and to graduate cum laude with her bachelor's degree and magna cum laude with the master's and doctor's degree. Again, she gives glory to God for she says, *"[lowliness] elevates ambition into a virtue, a spur that makes us struggle. It is heaven's own incentive to make purpose great and achievement greater."*

Life became rewarding and adventurous for many years. Married to a medical doctor, she enjoys telling how she conquered the fear of flying by purchasing a Piper Cherokee 180 HP and in four weeks earning her license. She continued to upgrade—Commercial Pilot, Multi-engine and Instrument Rating, Certified Flight/Instrument/ Ground Instructor, and eventually Senior Flight Instructor for the Civil Air Patrol. She not only flew her husband to medical meetings across the United States, but she also flew members of her First Baptist Sunday School class (some very elderly) to places they could never go by car! The culmination, perhaps, of all this preparation was being able to take part in international races, piloting the Goodyear Blimp, and serving three terms on both Alabama's Aeronautics Commission and Montgomery Airport Authority!

But then Dr. Relfe's life changed. In 1976, the Lord spoke to Mary: *"Set your house in order. I'm going to take your husband."* Two month's later, Dr. C. B. Relfe was diagnosed with leukemia. Dr. Mary Relfe said, *"With much prayer and fasting for his life, the Lord spoke again: **'Fear not, for I have redeemed thee, I have called thee by My name, thou art Mine…thou art married to Me'.**"* Mary prayed again, *"Lord, is this what You mean: I'm to be married to You, called by Your name, forgo any social life and in essence, become like a eunuch for the kingdom of heaven's sake, as You describe in Matthew 19:12?"* Twenty-five months later, God took her husband. Soon He took Flo, her nanny of many years, and shortly afterward, Anthony, her only child.

For two or three years after that, Dr. Relfe did little but read God's Word, pray, and study. *"Prime time at night was prayer time."* And then began the birthing of a new family. Calls started coming in: to teach on Far Eastern Broadcasting Company, to speak in China at a large Buddhists school for girls (*Many crowded into the auditorium "to see a woman who drove an airplane"*). God replaced her immediate family, taken between 1978-1980, with a huge extended family—mothers, fathers, sisters, brothers—knit together in an alliance He named *League of Prayer.*

After God gave a vision to Dr. Relfe about starting a new ministry, she invited Dr. Paul Yonggi Cho to come to the United States to help launch a prayer effort to call America back to prayer. In the most interesting circumstances orchestrated by God, Dr. Cho rearranged his schedule and accepted the invitation: "Booked at another place, he was going to decline when the Holy Spirit spoke: *'Go to the prayer closet and pray about this invitation.'* Upon kneeling to pray, God gave him a vision of me [Dr. Relfe] in this work. He said: *'Lord, I don't know this person, and I have a program scheduled in another place.'* The Lord said to him: *'Shove your program aside. This is My program'."* Thus, Dr. Cho flew to the U.S. and The League of Prayer ministry was "initiated" in 1985.

Besides being the head of The League of Prayer (headquartered in Alabama), traveling to speaking engagements, and writing, Dr. Mary Relfe overseas the League of Prayer Altar where many are healed. With the help of "a few dedicated folk," League of Prayer works and witnesses in the ghettos of Montgomery with food, clothes, and financial assistance; goes into hundreds of prisons in Alabama, Russia, Siberia and Ukraine; provides food for refugees fleeing from Albania and Bosnia; makes mission trips into Japan, Taiwan and Korea; ministers to multitudes in Russia with Bibles, food, clothes, and medicines; builds homes and schools and supplies a water system and hundreds of latrines for families in Honduras, the Philippines, Cambodia, and more recently, for victims of the tsunami in Sri Lanka and Indonesia. *"Heaven only has a record of how many orphans and abandoned ones"* they have assisted. Dr. Relfe uses no high-profile means to access the masses--as TV, radio, magazine, or website-- and each year *"God bears witness"* through her Auditor and others that He can trust Dr. Relfe. Steve Richardson, CPA, said, *"I have never seen operational efficiencies such as exist at The League. Administrative costs are the lowest of any nonprofit's expenses I have ever seen. Of all the charities I audit, none reach the ethical standard of League of Prayer."*

Throughout her life, Dr. Relfe has received various healings, but at the age of twenty-seven she received an unusual, miraculous healing. She calls it an operation in heaven by God! Future generations should be jolted to great faith in God by reading her encounter. Awakened one morning with one side of her body paralyzed and symptoms pointing to a brain tumor, she cried out to God. The night before her appointment with a neurologist, Dr. Relfe had plans to pray all night but fell asleep and in a dream or vision entered Chicago

Medical Observatory. *"Surgeons and nurses in their operating gowns surrounded my bed. The primary surgeon said to me, 'We are going to open up your head and look on your brain'. With his finger he traced the incision he would make."* She went to sleep, a double sleep!

Awakening back in her room (still asleep and in a vision) the surgeon standing over her said, *"We have removed your scalp, looked at your brain, and there is nothing growing on it."* She then awoke in her own bed and said, *"Lord, you rearranged my appointment with a heavenly neurologist."* While wondering if she should keep her appointment with the earthly neurologist, the phone rang, and the assistant told Mary the doctor had an emergency. They would have to re-schedule. Dr. Relfe had already had heavenly surgery; re-scheduling was unnecessary for she had already been healed, and that was "many more than twenty-seven years ago"!

As a "stone of remembrance," Dr. Relfe tells how she approaches God for healing (or for any need): *"Failure to first seek God's divine intervention in any sickness carries a high degree of risk."*

In II Chronicles 16:12-13 King Asa was *"diseased in his feet, until his disease was exceeding great, yet in his disease he sought not to the Lord, but to physicians. And Asa slept with his fathers and died...."*

This has been Dr. Relfe's pattern and precedent: *"prayer, fasting, persevering, quoting scriptures that under gird my requests, searching my life, humbling myself, drawing back from secular pursuits as reading newspapers, watching the news, increasing my giving and making oft inquiries of the Lord [pleading with God to answer]. I consulted with myself (making sure everything was well with my soul). Then I went to see a physician."*

"Therefore know that the Lord your God,
He is God,
the faithful God
who keeps covenant and mercy
for a thousand generations
with those who love Him
and Keep His commandments;
and He repays those who hate Him
to their face, to destroy them."
--Deuteronomy 7:9

GOD'S GRACE

"Cheap grace is the grace we bestow on ourselves. Cheap grace is the preaching of forgiveness without requiring repentance, baptism without church discipline, Communion without confession. Cheap grace is grace without discipleship, grace without the cross, grace without Jesus Christ, living and incarnate." --Dietrich Bonhoeffer*

"I really only love God as much as I love the person I love the least."-- Dorothy Day

---

"Many years ago I was driven to the conclusion that the two major causes of most emotional problems among evangelical Christians are these: the failure to understand, receive, and live out God's unconditional grace and forgiveness; and the failure to give out that unconditional love, forgiveness, and grace to other people.... We read, we hear, we believe a good theology of grace. But that's not the way we live. The good news of the Gospel of grace has not penetrated the level of our emotions."

-- David Seamands *

To love a person," said Dostoevsky, "means to see him as God intended him to be."

*"No word in English carries a greater possibility of terror than the little word 'as' in the Lord's Prayer. What makes the 'as' so terrifying? The fact that Jesus plainly links our **forgiven-ness** by the Father with our **forgiving-ness** of fellow human beings. Jesus' next remark could not be more explicit: 'If you do not forgive men their sins, your Father will not forgive your sins'."* --Charles Williams

The next participant, Philip Yancey, wrote the best seller *What's So Amazing About Grace* that is referred to in his encounter. He stresses that repentance is the doorway to grace: *"If I understand the story correctly about the sinful woman in John 8* [caught in adultery], *she is the one nearest the kingdom of God. Indeed, I can* *only advance in the kingdom if I become like that woman: trembling, humbled, without excuse, my palms open to receive God's grace. The stance of openness to receive is what I call the 'catch' to grace. It must be received, and the Christian term for that act is repentance, the doorway to grace."*—Philip Yancey

---

MR. PHILIP YANCEY

As a writer, I work in isolation. My greatest joy, truly, happens when I connect with readers at a deep level. I wrote the book What's So Amazing About Grace out of my own experiences of what I call "Ungrace." In response I've received thousands of letters from people who tell me their own stories of encountering God's amazing grace. It heals family wounds, leads to forgiveness and reconciliation, even brings salve to wounds caused by the church. I never imagined this flood when I wrote the book. It assures me that grace - not hate, not violence - is the mightiest force in the universe.

Philip Yancey

PHILIP YANCEY

As a writer, I work in isolation. My greatest joy, truly, happens when I connect with readers at a deep level. I wrote the book <u>What's So Amazing About Grace</u> out of my own experiences of what I call "Ungrace." In response I've received thousands of letters from people who tell me their own stories of encountering God's amazing grace. It heals family wounds, leads to forgiveness and reconciliation, even brings salve to wounds caused by the church. I never imagined this flood when I wrote the book. It assures me that grace—not hate, not violence—is the mightiest force in the universe.

Philip Yancey

Philip Yancey
"Journalistic Defender of the Faith"

Our generation remembers Philip Yancey for giving us books that stretch our imagination, for providing answers to difficult questions, and for reaffirming our hope in Jesus Christ. Reared during the hippie generation, disillusioned by the Church world, Yancey went through a period of "reacting against everything" he had been taught as a child. He found his way back to faith and "writes," as he states, "for those who have been hurt or burned by the church."

If you could pretend you had gathered for a night to remember Philip Yancey some of the guests would have said the following:

Billy Graham*: "There is no writer in the evangelical world that I admire and appreciate more."*

Lewis B. Smedes*, Fuller Theological Seminary: "Yancey's book **The Jesus I Never Knew** took away my blinders...until I saw the Savior anew and thought I heard Him ask me, 'Now who do you say I am?'"*

Paul Harvey*: "By the time I got to the end of **Where is God When It Hurts**? my heart was crying out, 'Thank you, God, for pain'."*

Joni Eareckson Tada*: Sometimes "pain and paralysis seem to push away the presence of God." Philip helps us "find out exactly where God really is when it hurts."*

Mark O. Hatfield*: "One of the most gifted writers of our day has put a telescope on the brilliant star of grace and finely focused on what a beautiful and powerful healing force followers of Jesus Christ could become."*

Philip Yancey, journalist and award-winning author, earned graduate degrees in Communications and English from Wheaton College Graduate School and the University of Chicago. In 1971, he joined the staff of Campus Life Magazine, serving there as Editor for eight years. Since 1978, Yancey has primarily concentrated on freelance writing with more than 600 of his articles appearing in 80 different publications, including *Reader's Digest, National Wildlife,*

Saturday Evening Post, and **Christian Century**. In 1983, editors of *Christianity Today* asked him to write a monthly column.

Yancey's twenty books include ***Where Is God When It Hurts?***, ***The Student Bible***, and ***Disappointment with God***. Christian bookstore managers selected ***The Jesus I Never Knew*** as the 1996 Book of the Year, and ***What's So Amazing About Grace?*** won the same award in 1998. His most recent books are ***Rumors of Another World, Reaching for the Invisible God***, and ***Soul Survivor.***

Philip Yancey grew up in a strict, fundamental home and church in the Deep South. When he was one year old, his father died after being advised by his church leaders to take himself off the iron lung machine, assuring him he would be healed. Yancey admits that much of the work of his adult life has been spent in recovering from the injustices he saw and experienced as a child. Coming to terms with himself and with God has contributed to his successful writing career and to his international influence.

The day after graduating from high school near Atlanta, Georgia, Philip began a summer job digging ditches. There he learned that whites drank the cool clean water and the blacks drank another type. Born in Atlanta, Georgia, *"five years before the Supreme Court ruled in favor of integrated schools, fifteen years before a civil rights law forced restaurants and motels to serve all races...,"* Yancey saw the worst of apartheid conditions in society and in the church. He said, *"They preached racism from the pulpit and were preoccupied...with measuring skirts and hair."* He has repented many times for his own racism sometimes wondering if most of the problems in our society (drugs, changing values, systemic poverty, and the breakdown of the nuclear family) are *"consequences of a deeper, underlying cause: our centuries-old sin of racism."*

Yancey has a distinct, brilliant style of writing. He loves words and their meanings, and as one reviewer said, "He is the thinking man's friend." Yancey says, *"I have learned that all I offer, all that any writer can offer, is a point of view. As I write about people, I find myself honing in on the sense of irony that almost defines our species. Human beings, including myself, seem odd to me. Half-animal, half-angel, we keep surprising and disappointing ourselves and each other. I write books to resolve things that are bothering me, things I don't have answers to.... So, I tend to tackle different problems related to faith, things of concern to me, things I wonder about and worry about.... I tend to go back to the Bible as a model, because I don't know a more honest book.   I can't think of any argument against God that isn't already included in the Bible.... Theologically, I...have a thirst for God, a reverence for the Bible, and a love for Jesus."*

Philip Yancey and wife Janet lived in downtown Chicago for many years before moving to a very different environment in Colorado. In his books he refers often to the influence an inner city church in Chicago had on his "way back to faith." At one point he taught a Sunday school class there, using videotapes on the life of Jesus. This activity ultimately led to the book *The Jesus I Never Knew.*

As a journalist Yancey has lived a colorful life traveling, researching, writing, and being chosen to appear on panels to defend his faith. He has interviewed diverse people ('stars' and servants, and he prefers servants) and has been invited worldwide to observe and take part in social and political changes.

Since he writes "openly about matters of faith," Yancey was once chosen along with a representative from Harvard Divinity School to serve on a panel at a conference in South Carolina addressing the topic "Faith and Physics." Yancey followed an atheist who had begun by saying he had no use for religion. When Yancey's turn came to speak, *"I acknowledged the mistakes the church had made and thanked them for not burning us Christians at the stake.... I also thanked them for rigorous honesty about their own nontheistic point of view."* He then read from Chet Raymo, an astronomer, who had calculated the odds of our universe resulting from sheer chance. The tension was diffused.

A prodigious researcher and gifted with an inquiring mind, Yancey shifts back and forth in his books telling many people's story in order to reinforce his point. What does the Bible say about hope, about suffering, about God's attitude toward us?   For example, in *Where Is God When It Hurts*? he weaves the viewpoint of Luther and Calvin, Bunyan and Donne, God and Job, C. S. Lewis and G. K Chesterton, Peter De Vries, Dr. Paul Brand, Elie Wiesel and Corrie ten Boom, and hundreds of others! He is a classical scholar and enjoys playing classical music on the piano. He travels abroad at least four times a year. He quotes from the classics, from modern literature, and from the Bible. Seemingly, nothing is left out! And he is a good man for he loves the mountains! He finds a "strange thrill in wildness" (dashing down to the safety of timberline...as lightning bolts strike closer) and says, "*I feel most comfortable alone, on a summer day, hiking up a 14,000-foot mountain with none but the marmots and pikas to keep me company.*"

He tackles tough questions that most people block from their minds or about which they become angry and blame God or the Church. His books are like reading a classic, probing ideas that perhaps C. S. Lewis wouldn't even touch.

One man asked Yancey if God would forgive the sin he was about to commit (leaving his wife for a younger woman). With great wisdom Yancey replied: Will God forgive what you are about to do? Of course, He will. Read your Bible. David. Peter. Paul— "*God builds His church on the backs of people who murder, commit adultery, deny Him, and persecute His followers.*" But.... "*Because of Christ, forgiveness is now our problem, not God's. What we have to go through to commit sin distances us from God—we change in the very act of rebellion—and there is no guarantee we will come back. You ask me about forgiveness now, but will you even want it later, especially if it involves repentance.*"

The form used to organize *I Was Just Wondering* (a book, he says, of many questions and a few answers) is typical of Yancey's journalistic style of writing. Some of the tantalizing questions asked are:

1) What would happen in the national consensus if these nine words came to mind when you said the word "Christian": love, joy, peace, patience, kindness, goodness, faithfulness, gentleness, and self-control?
2) Why do sinners feel so attracted to Jesus but so repulsed by the church?
3) Would Christians support a national Prohibition movement against the major health hazard of obesity?
4) What would a truly Christian hospital look like?
5) Why did God stay silent during the Holocaust?
6) What is God like? How is it that most theology books portray Him as logical, orderly, unchanging, and ineffable, whereas

the Bible portrays Him as emotional, flexible, vulnerable, and, above all, passionate?

7) What would make the whole world believe in Jesus?

In one encounter in "The Midnight Church," Yancey attends an AA meeting with a friend who admits that AA has replaced the church for him, a fact that sometimes troubles him. When Yancey asked the friend to "name the one quality missing in the local church that AA had somehow provided," the friend quietly said, "dependency." He continued, *"None of us can make it on our own—isn't that why Jesus came? Yet most church people give off a self-satisfied air of piety or superiority. I don't sense them consciously leaning on God or each other. Their lives appear to be in order."* He continued, *"What I hate most about myself, was the one thing God used to bring me back to him. Because of it, I know I can't survive without him. Maybe that's the redeeming value of alcoholics.* ***Maybe God is calling us alcoholics to teach the saints what it means to be dependent on him and on his community on earth."***

Where Is God When It Hurts*? was first written in the mid-1970's ("at an age when I had no right to tackle the daunting problem of pain") and revised in 1990. "For a good portion of my life,"* Yancey says, *"I shared the perspective of those who rail against God for allowing pain.... I could find no way to rationalize a world as toxic as this one. As I visited those with leprosy, particularly, I became aware of pain's underlying value.* (The sensation of pain is a gift—the gift that nobody wants.)" It is a communication network. *"Without pain, our lives would be fraught with danger, and devoid of many basic pleasures.... My anger about pain has melted mostly for one reason: I have come to know God. He has given me joy and love and happiness and goodness...they have been enough to convince me that my God is worthy of trust."*

In researching the root of the word "grace" or "charis" in Greek, Yancey explains that it means *"rejoice, I am glad,"* but he questions whether or not *"rejoicing and gladness"* are the first images that come to mind in most of our churches. One person quipped, *"Church? Why should I go there? I was already feeling terrible about myself. They'd just make me feel worse."* He points out that the attitude of many in our churches is upside down. Some sins that Jesus taught against are condoned, yet we shun the drug addict, the alcoholic, the prostitute, the homosexual, the poor. He emphasizes that *"God has given the church a mandate of representing His love to a suffering world,"* but too often the church turns people away.

Where is God when it hurts? Yancey answers by launching into a divinely inspired poetic explanation:

"He has been there from the beginning, designing a pain system that, even in the midst of a fallen world, still bears the stamp of His genius and equips us for life on this planet.

"He transforms pain, using it to teach and strengthen us, if we allow it to turn us toward Him.

"With great restraint, He watches this rebellious planet live on, in mercy allowing the human project to continue in its self-guided way.

"He lets us cry out, like Job, in loud fits of anger against Him, blaming Him for a world we spoiled.

"He allies himself with the poor and suffering, founding a kingdom tilted in their favor. He stoops to conquer.

"He promises supernatural help to nourish the spirit, even if our physical suffering goes unrelieved.

"He has joined us. He has hurt and bled and cried and suffered. He has dignified for all time those who suffer, by sharing their pain.

"He is with us now, ministering to us through his Spirit and through members of His body who are commissioned to bear us up and relieve our suffering for the sake of the Head.

"He is waiting, gathering the armies of good. One day He will unleash them, and the world will see one last terrifying moment of suffering before the full victory is ushered in. Then, God will create for us a new, incredible world. And pain shall be no more (I Corinthians 15:51-55)."

When asked about catastrophes, the aids epidemic, or tsunamis, he reminds us that Jesus seems to imply (taken from Luke 13:1-5, *"... unless you repent you will all likewise perish."*) that we bystanders of these events *"have as much to learn from the event as do the sufferers themselves."* Instead of blaming or questioning God, we should learn humility and gratitude that God has withheld judgment; we should be called to repentance, to "be ready" in case we are the next victims. In his travels overseas, Yancey notices a striking difference in the way Christians pray. In affluent countries Christians tend to pray, *"Lord, take this trial away from us."* In poor countries Christians pray, *"Lord, give us the strength to bear this trial."*

After Yancey did a study on "God's favorites," he says they are not immune from times of testing. Saints become saints by somehow clinging to the stubborn conviction that God deserves our trust, even when it looks like the world is caving in. After his moral failures, King David intentionally involved God in every detail of his life and confidently knew he mattered to God. *"When I finished my study of God's favorites, one fact stood out above all others,"* Yancey remarks. *"Those people hardly resembled the healthy, prosperous, pampered saints I hear described on religious television. The contrast was striking, and it puzzled me for a time. Perhaps here is the difference: religious television must concern itself with pleasing an audience of thousands, even millions. God's favorites are singularly devoted to pleasing an audience of just **One**."*

In **Soul Survivor,** Yancey listens to a taxi driver relate his story about the Twin Towers massacre. Yancey remarks: *"I have never been especially patriotic. I've traveled too much overseas, I guess, and have seen from afar the arrogance and insensitivity of the United States. Sometimes I envy my friends who travel with a Canadian, rather than an American, passport. Our military, our Olympic athletes, even our tourists, walk with a swagger...."* However, he says September 11 changed his attitude after he heard Congress sing "God Bless America" and as he listened to the Buckingham Palace guard play "The Star-Spangled Banner." He then realized that the United States is the land of promise and potential.

Philip Yancey talks about the persecuted church in other countries and the spoiled, compromising church in America. With friend Ron Nikkel, head of Prison Fellowship International, Yancey took a writing assignment to visit prisons in Chile and Peru, South America. What he found should encourage the reader:

Marxists, Muslims, Hindus and secular humanists fail at their prisons. But they let prison ministries in, and there behind bars in the least likely of all places the church of God takes shape. *"It's New Testament church in its purest form,"* says Yancey. *"All distinctions of denominations, race, and class are gone."* Instead of 5,000 different denominations and church groups, in prisons, the Christians are one. And even in the decadent United States (which has a higher percentage of prisoners than any other nation), *"the church is showing signs of life—the church behind bars, that is."* In one prison former terrorists now take Communion alongside Protestants they had once sworn to kill. Of course, we don't hear or read about such events in the news.

It is impossible to do justice to Philip Yancey! (You must read the description of Yancey's two conversions in **Rumors of Another World**—conversions from the natural world to the supernatural and later a rediscovery of the natural from a new viewpoint!). For now, the recorder chooses to end the sketch with Yancey's description of Jesus from the book **The Jesus I Never Knew**! Yancey says, *"...Jesus is radically unlike anyone else who has ever lived. The difference* (in Charles Williams' words) *is the difference between 'one who is an example of living and one who is the life itself'."* Yancey describes **Jesus as**:

"**A Sinless Friend of Sinners**. *Demons recognized him, the sick flocked to him, and sinners doused his feet and head with perfume."* He revealed himself as Messiah first to a Samaritan woman who had a history of failed marriages; in His last breath, Jesus pardoned a thief. Yet Jesus was not a sinner.

"**The God-Man**. He gave us himself in the form of a person. 'I am the way.' 'I forgive your sins.' 'I am sending you prophets and wise men and teachers'—He the sovereign God of history. 'I and the Father are one.' 'Anyone who has seen me has seen the Father!' (Imagine Buddha or Mohammed, Socrates or Marx making such statements)."

"**A Portrait of God**. *The Apostle Paul called Jesus 'the image of the invisible God.' Jesus was God's exact replica: 'For God was pleased to have all his fullness dwell in Him'.*" Yancey further describes him as *"brilliant, untamed, tender, creative, slippery, irreducible, paradoxically humble—Jesus stands up to scrutiny. He is who I want my God to be. Jesus brought God near.... Jesus brought the message that God cares for the grass of the field, feeds the sparrows, numbers the hairs on a person's head.... Too easily we forget what it cost Jesus to win for us all—ordinary people, not just priests—immediate access to God's presence."*

"**The Lover**. (Yancey says on his own he would come up with a very different notion of God.) *My God would be static, unchanging; I would not conceive of God 'coming' and 'going'. My God would control all things with power, stamping out opposition swiftly and decisively. Jesus reveals a God who comes in search of us, a God who makes room for our freedom even when it costs the Son's life, a God who is vulnerable. Above all, Jesus reveals a God who is love. On our own, would any of us come up with the notion of a God who loves and yearns to be loved?"* *("It would be eccentric for anyone to claim that he loved Zeus or that Zeus loved a human being....")* In startling contrast, the Christian Bible affirms, "God is love," and cites love as the main reason Jesus came to earth: *"This is how God showed his love among us: He sent his one and only Son into the world that we might live through him."*--1 John 4:10

Our generation is blessed to have a journalist and author who seeks truth and leads other people to truth. We are grateful he did not become a "Judas dropout" (Do you suppose the disciples were without flaw?). Instead Philip Yancey took the high road, and in the manner of the Apostle Paul, he used his hurts to understand the hurts of others. To remain faithful to God was a deliberate choice Yancey made! As was said by an African-American woman about Yancey's Chicago pastor, Bill Leslie, *"Our generation is grateful for a man sent from God"* (to those who have been hurt by other Christians or to those who *"are living in the borderlands of faith"*) whose name is Philip!

"Though the fig tree may not blossom,
Nor fruit be on the vines;
Though the labor of the olive may fail,
And the fields yield no food;
Though the flock may be cut off
from the fold,
And there be no herd in the stalls—
Yet I will rejoice in the Lord,
I will joy in the God of my salvation.
The Lord God is my strength;
He will make my feet
like deer's feet,
And He will make me walk
on my high hills."

--Habakkuk 3:17-19

"Think often on God, by day, by night, in your business, and even in your diversions.
He is always near you and with you; LEAVE HIM NOT ALONE.
You would think it rude to leave a friend alone who came to visit you; why, then, must God be neglected."
--Brother Lawrence

THE RECORDER

The Recorder's Encounter

In a supernatural way, I was led to research material and read one of the participants books that related to a need I had at that moment or to baggage I had dragged with me for a lifetime! Instead of reading about and working on a participants entry in alphabetical order God led me to a problem area in my life, and with His grace and the experience of the participant, I was moved to love God and to have an intimate love for and friendship with Jesus. In fact, the last person to participate in the project contacted me almost two years after the original requests were mailed; "Was it too late to submit a 'God encounter'?" God used her life to complete the biggest need in my life: to really, really love God and to know His voice. God put me in His classroom, took me back to "basics" and if I could choose a different title for the book, it simply would be Christianity 101!

For my nephew and niece,

ZeeZee

God Put Me In His Classroom!

The Recorder's Encounter

I love looking at old manuscripts. My visits to museums in Europe attest to that, and I believe I know the looks of Jesus' handwritten note in the sand!

To handwrite a note communicates that you care and when a word of encouragement is written for another person, *"it is often **perceived to be more genuine** than when it is spoken."* So some of the great minds have said! After I read about this type of research, a dream or desire began to form in my heart to collect handwritten "God encounters" of great people of faith, add a list of their achievements, and publish the results. As for the time this plan would take: no more than two or three fortnights!

But God had other plans! God put me in His classroom. The classroom was designed just for me, taught and guided by Holy Spirit and great people of faith, and I became not only the student but also the student teacher. The recorder's greatest encounter with God has been in putting the material together for this book, and alas, it is now almost three years later than the "fortnight"! However, God's timing is perfect!

E. W. Bullinger's Number in Scripture discloses the importance of the number seventy. Seventy (7 x 10) is significant, for the number "signifies perfect spiritual order carried out with all spiritual power and significance." Thus, to reassure His love for one person, God created a book to be published maybe on <u>my 70th birthday</u>--or in a fortnight!

Several friends advised me to include my "God encounter" relating the summer incident when many chartered planes were canceled from flying out of Europe (one of which was my flight). From England to Holland to Germany, I was mysteriously moved but stranded for two weeks. In Frankfurt, Germany, an extremely large, tall man (I believe to have been an angel), who instantly disappeared before I could question or thank him, handed me an athletic pass (the origin of which we could never locate) enabling me to board a military flight out of Europe. However, my recent experience eclipses the natural rescue and I would rather tell about a greater spiritual rescue made by the sovereign God of the universe who took a special interest in one person.

In an uncanny, no doubt supernatural way, I was led to research material and read one of the participant's books that related to a need I had at that moment or to baggage I had dragged with me for a lifetime! Instead of reading about and working on a participant's entry in alphabetical order, God led me to a problem area in my life, and with His grace and the experience of the participant, I was moved to love God and to have an intimate love for and friendship with Jesus. In fact, the last person to participate in the project contacted me almost two years after the original requests were mailed. *"Was it too late to submit a 'God Encounter'?"* God used her life to complete the biggest need in my life: to really, really love God and to know His voice. God put me in His classroom, took me back to "basics" and if I could choose a different title for the book, it simply would be *Christianity 101*!

John 15:7 records, *"If you abide in Me, and My Words abide in you, you shall ask what you will, and it shall be done unto you."* The word "done" in Hebrew means "created." The "you" refers to me (or to you!) and me alone. If I abide in Him and His Words abide in me, His love is so great He will even create for me (or anyone else fulfilling the command to abide) that for which I ask. Such a promise is great personal, individual love from the Father of the universe! He created a book with testimonies from people of great faith to jolt me out of my apathy—just for me. My prayer is that *other* people, too, will be awakened from apathy and experience a new love for Jesus the Savior.

I have related this for my relatives--in my own handwriting--to give it a personal touch and to prove its authenticity!

For my nephew and niece,
ZeeZee

THE RECORDER
(For My Parents' Descendants)

The greatest blessing that can come to a person is to be born in America and reared in a Christian home. I had the greatest of foundations! I grew up with many happy memories as a child, mainly of being on the front seat in a church—struggling to stay awake, or being jostled across miles and miles from one church service or camp-meeting to another. This was the 1940's and 1950's and my parents were evangelists. I met many people, played in the fields with other kids during "camp-meeting" services, poured water down holes to drive tarantulas from their homes, and formed friendships, only to be ripped apart as we drove on to another town, another church.

Our home was blessed to have ministers and singing groups spend a night or two as they passed through town, for this was an era before motels and hotels flourished and when people were just coming through the Great Depression. Dr. C. B. Cox, Superintendent of the Church of the Nazarene Colorado District, taught me how to play tennis, Dr J. A. Phillips was a frequent visitor, and also Dr. Haldor Lilleness of Lillenas (music) Publications. In later years, I have wondered why some of the people visited, but alas, I was too young at the time to be interested. Because music was so important (Mother played the piano, organ, accordion, violin), our home was a fun place, apparently, for this entourage.

For my parents' descendents, I include an important stone of remembrance about my sister. Leonora studied "voice" and while in college traveled with a trio and sang on a radio program (before TV days) broadcasting from Nampa, Idaho. Since she died young, she is now singing in heaven, but as she was leaving this world she raised herself up and said, "See! See! O! It's so beautiful!"

A stone of remembrance about my father: He was a man of prayer, and even in his latter years, in a weakened condition, he was always faithful to church. Asked to lead in prayer at church, he prayed with the voice of a young man!

For a time I had a tender heart and anytime an altar call was given, I was one of the first to go forward. I don't know my age, or the date, but I suppose I gave my heart to Jesus Christ before I was ten years old. At times my sister and I were left at the Brizendine's home or with my favorite aunt and uncle. But too many times my parents left. One time as I stood in the yard waving goodbye, inwardly with clinched teeth, I said to myself, "I will never show emotion again; I will never love anyone again." A hardness settled in: I became stoic on the outside, and literally expressed little outward emotion until fifty-plus years later—with the gathering of the material for this project. Probably one of the greatest influences in understanding a "hard heart" was the book written by Doug and Laura Lee Oldham, *There Is Hope*. God gives us a choice and wrong choices can lead to hard heartedness.

About my mother: Known by many for her great sense of humor, she "never met a stranger." She was devoted, passionate for Jesus. My fondest memories were the "jam sessions" we had even in later years when I would return home--she at the piano and the recorder at the organ. After I became a disjointed teenage octopus, the saddest encounter we had occurred as my mother said, "Your father and I were doing what we thought God required. We were obeying God, but had we known you would be so affected by our obedience we would have chosen to "go to hell." I suppose this remembrance is the reason for the compassion, now, in my heart for all leaders who are giving their lives for the Gospel's sake.

That also is the reason I learned to love and appreciate each person who used <u>rationed</u> time to write of his or her God encounter!

(Eventually, due to my father's illness, my parents left the evangelistic circuit and Mother became successful working for the court system in El Paso County, Colorado.)

My thought process has not been to believe that God really loved me; I believed John 3:16 ("for God so loved the world"), but I believed He loved others and I was just one of many! Since hearing John Hagee's wife, Diana, confess to the same feeling, I have been comforted! With so many one-parent or broken families, many exist with this deeply ingrained fault, desperately in need of the healing touch of Jesus Christ.

Therapy and prayer sometimes cannot release childhood damage. As I read Gene Edward's Divine Romance, my heart softened. I came to believe how much God loves me, each individual, and longs for a reciprocal response. ("All I wanted was their love," God said in the *Divine Romance*.)   Mentally I came to know that God and Jesus are one, and as one participant said, "They are not somewhere out in space, but by Their Spirit, They live within me!" I began practicing the Presence of Christ, telling God how much I love Him—for that is all He really desires—and love for Christ began to grow. Gradually I knew I was/am special to Him!

I am sometimes chickenhearted! As I gathered material for the book project and read that a prophecy had been given by a reputable man saying that 70% of Christians sitting in Churches today would miss the rapture, I was shaken, rattled, unnerved by the teaching. I know the argument of some theologians that a person can sin and confess the sin and God will forgive; however, if a person who knows the Gospel misses the "taking away," the rapture, **there is the possibility** he will go through the tribulation. **I don't want to take that chance.** The Scripture rather plainly states that Christ is returning, not for those doing their own thing, but for those who are watching and waiting for Him and for those whose lamps are trimmed and prepared.

I am also a late bloomer. I am aware of God's protection all of my life. However, it was late in my life, after reading about the importance of commitment and surrender to Jesus Christ from Mrs. Anita Hashim, that a real confrontation began. Why are people so fearful of totally surrendering their life to Jesus Christ? D.L. Moody stated, *"There are very few in their hearts who do not believe in God, but what they will not do is give Him exclusive right-of-way. They are not ready to promise full allegiance to God alone."* This type of person occupies Church pews and I was one of them!

Finally, in a mall parking lot I stopped and said, "All right, God, I surrender everything; totally possess me." That surrender was difficult, but it was **the most logical thing I ever did.** Though active in church musings, serving and doing, paying tithes and giving offerings, I had been spiritually blind. There was a reserve, a self-sufficiency, a desire to be in control. I learned from Merlin Carothers and Don Gossett that when we begin thanking and praising God for **everything**, then God can direct every detail of our lives. What more could a person desire, knowing that God made the choice to be **all** things to us. (Letting God be in control is not a "cop-out"; this surrender means using pure wisdom.) Life has become so much more interesting!

In putting the biographical sketch together for Dr. Mary Ruth Swope, I realized I had been caught up in seeking secular rewards and degrees much as she had. After attending a church college, I transferred to the University of Colorado for graduate studies leading to an M.A. in British and American literature. The first day on campus the advisor laughingly said as he looked at my transcript, "We will destroy your faith here." And they did—for a time!

From Mrs. Joy Dawson I learned about the fear of God and how faith is increased, not only from hearing the Word, but also **by knowing about the character of God**. Many in this generation have lost that fear and respect of God. Cheap grace, free will, freedom, secularism, materialism, self-sufficiency, pride, pure rebellion short circuit many of us in America and we become spiritually blind. I learned from Mrs. Dawson and Dr. Swope about praying and waiting for an answer. (To wait two hours in one sitting to hear God's answer to a question was foreign to me.) From Jill Austin I was made aware that a person really, really can hear from God, and suddenly one day during the process, Dr. Relfe's comment "registered" that "prayer **is** a dialogue, not a monologue." How I longed to have been like some of the participants whose lives had been spent from early youth developing an intimate friendship with Christ! **Now**, that friendship and fellowship are developing and prayer becomes a pure delight!

Other issues I was forced to confront. When one totally surrenders, then warfare enters. The devil becomes threatened and aroused when he sees a "nominal Christian" energized by truth. Any dream brought to fruition can be compared to the natural birthing process and the devil was not interested in having the stories of the people in this book told. There were many obstacles: computer malfunction, —the devil really does mess with computers if he wishes to block Truth--broken scan disk and losing much of the material, personal illness, misunderstandings.

So I learned the importance of prayer and fasting, of thanking and praising and worshiping and right confession **based on a Verse,** not on transcendental meditation, which was emphasized in the educational world, but on a Scripture from the Bible. Finally, **I am a late bloomer** because I am just now learning about the force of love and grace. Philip Yancey's books had great influence. I had been through what Jill Austin calls the "killing fields of the church." But now it is okay! My focus is on Jesus Christ.

For every person who may have been detoured in life (by circumstances or by sin), God magnificently provides a place for him, and this **new** understanding **has given me a greater love for God. Would Allah, or Buddha, or Mohammed take such loving care of each individual? God's answer: "Is there a God besides Me? I know not one--**Isaiah 44:8."** (What a sense of humor from the One who made the universe!)

One of the great realities of Christianity is we have Jesus Christ who takes pity on mankind, heals him, and gives him a promise and hope of eternal life. **He tells us He loves us** ("For God so loved the world that He gave His only begotten Son,—John 3:16") and **we can reciprocate that love,**

> *"Oh God, You are my God; early will I seek You;*
> *My soul thirsts for You;*
> *My flesh longs for You...*
> *Because Your loving kindness is better than life,*
> *My lips shall praise You,*
> *Thus will I bless You while I live;*
> *I will lift up my hands in Your name—Psalm 63:1-4."*

Can you imagine the four-faced, four-armed Hindu god Brahma (born in a golden egg) **telling you he loves you?**

Or imagine the many sects of Buddhism, who often stress "find God in yourself;" life is about suffering, so be a lamp unto your own feet. In other words, **there is no God to tell you He loves you nor any God to tell him you love Him?**

Jeremiah 10:23—*"O Lord, I know the way of man is not in himself; it is not in man who walks to direct his own steps."*

Or imagine the one god of Islam (**no Son, no Holy Spirit**), **no one to die for your sins, no redeemer for mankind**.

Or imagine the Absolute Tao (of Taoism), an unknowable, transcendent reality **taking a personal interest in your sorrows or joys and telling you that he loves you.**

307

Imagine one of these gods praying for you as Jesus Christ did in Luke 22:32, **"But I have prayed for you**, that your faith should not fail,..." "And I have declared to them Your name, and will declare it, that the love with which You loved Me may be in them, and I in them—John 17:26."

Yes, God has many characteristics, but the compassion of God convinced me! After meditating on these thoughts, the coldness in my heart melted and I came to love Jesus, that is, desperately love Jesus, the Savior of all of us, and I appreciate every participant in the book project for taking part in the rescue!

THIS HAPPENED IN MY GENERATION!
"You have made me exceedingly glad with Your presence —Psalm 21:6."

"Thus says the Lord,
the King of Israel, and his Redeemer,
the Lord of hosts;
'I am the Last;
besides Me there is no God.
And who can proclaim as I do?
Then let him declare it and set it in order for Me.
Since I appointed the ancient people,
and the things that are coming and shall come,
let them show these to them.
Do not fear, nor be afraid;
have I not told you from that time,
and declared it?
You are My witnesses.
Is there a God besides Me?
Indeed there is no other Rock;
I know not one'."

--Isaiah 44:6-8

Don't Forget To Remember!

"In a crisis, God can and will do it again!" --David Wilkerson

In the wilderness, **unbelief** angered God the most: *"Then the Lord said to Moses: 'How long will these people reject Me? And how long will they not **believe** Me, with all the signs which I have performed among them? I will strike them with the pestilence and disinherit them, and I will make of you a nation greater and mightier than they'*--Numbers 14:11,12.*"

God said in Deuteronomy 30:15-16, *"See, **I have set before you this day life and good**, death and evil. If you obey the commandments of the Lord your God...then you shall live and multiply, and the Lord your God will bless you in the land...."* We also are commanded to teach the things we have seen and heard about God to our children and our grandchildren *"that it may go well with you and with your children after you, and that you may prolong your days...Deuteronomy 4:40."*

We can almost see the heaving heart of God in Deuteronomy 5:29 when He says, *"Oh, that they had such a heart in them that they would fear Me and always keep all My commandments, that it might go well with them and their children forever."* With such a magnanimous offer, we wonder why **our generation** so easily forgets--just as the people of Israel so easily forgot--God's wondrous works and all of His power and might.

Dietrich Bonhoeffer said, *"Satan does not fill us with hatred of God but with forgetfulness of God."* We don't make plans to forget; distractions, cares of life, temptations, losing our "first love," and failing to spend time in prayer and reading His Word derail our attention from God. **When impossible, unsolvable situations occur, unless we are rooted in faith in God and with memories of how He delivered us in the past, we may panic and forget that God can and will deliver again.**

How **do** we usually react when an emergency arises? The disciples (in their twenties and thirties) were not having "senior moments" when they panicked after being told by Jesus to supply food for 4,000 men! Within a short span of months, they had witnessed two similar large-crowd-feeding miracles. But His disciples said to Him, *"Where could we get enough bread in the wilderness to fill such a great multitude* (Matthew 15:33)?" By **looking at seemingly impossible circumstances and feeling helpless,** they were reacting just as we do today. In our wilderness, where can we get enough to meet our needs and the needs of those around us?

Jesus said to them, *"Do you not yet understand, or remember the five loaves of the five thousand and how many baskets you took up? Nor the seven loaves of the four thousand and how many large baskets you took up* (Matthew 16:9-10)?" *"Why do you reason because you have no bread? Do you not yet perceive nor understand? Is your heart still **hardened**? Having eyes, do you not see? And having ears, do you not hear? And do you not remember? When I broke the five loaves for the five thousand, how many baskets full of fragments did you take up? How is it **you do not understand** (Mark 8:17-21)?"* How **could** they forget so soon?

Day after day, the disciples had walked with Jesus. We wonder, however, if they had faith, if they really believed God? Their memories should have engendered faith, but they did not understand that in their crisis **Jesus could do it again.** Hebrews 4:2 reminds us of the consequences: *"...the word which they heard did not profit them, not being mixed with faith in those who heard it."* Hebrews 3:12 labels an unbelieving heart as evil: *"Beware, brethren, lest there be in any of you an evil heart of unbelief in departing from the living God."* **To hear the gospel or to see the gospel in action is not enough; it must be believed.**

Scripture is replete with illustrations of men (and at least one woman, Eve!) who faced a dilemma or crisis, forgot God, but were restored. Adam faced a crisis of the will; David and Samson, moral crises; Peter a crisis of fear; and Jonah, an obedience crisis. Knowing the weakness of mankind and the tendency to forget so easily, perhaps God instituted the Communion Sacrament: "Do this in remembrance of Me." God knew about short-term memory, but He also knew the power of repetition.

Asaph **retells** the history of the Jewish nation in Psalm 78. To keep the people from making the same mistakes as their ancestors, the history was told over and over to each generation **so the faith** of each generation **would be rooted and grounded in God**. *"In spite of this they still sinned, and did not **believe** in His wondrous works. Therefore their days He consumed in futility, and their years in fear (Psalm 78:32). ...But He, being full of compassion, forgave their iniquity, and did not destroy them.... For He remembered that they were but flesh...(Psalm 78:38,39)."*

In Deuteronomy 6:5-9 God told Moses to tell the people, *"You shall love the Lord your God with all your heart, with all your soul, and with all your strength. And these words which I command you today shall be in your heart. You shall teach them diligently to your children, and shall talk of them when you sit in your house, when you walk by the way, when you lie down, and when you rise up. You shall bind them as a sign on your hand, and they shall be as frontlets* between your eyes. You shall write them on the door posts of your house and on your gates."*

Knowing how quickly people forget, God was telling them to protect and guard memories of their deliverances, keep them close at hand (as a sign on your hand), keep them in mind (as frontlets between your eyes). When they faced a crisis, an emergency, a dilemma, a heartache, an enemy, He was telling them to remember all the miracles He had done in the past.

For our generation we can keep a diary of our deliverances, those times God restored or delivered, and be sure to tell them to the children—when you sit around the dinner table and as you take trips. Together memorize Scripture verses. Place scripture posters in their room (I still remember the wall-hanging my mother placed in my room: *'In all your ways acknowledge Him, and He shall direct your paths'*). To a generation taught in ungodly schools, by ungodly movies, lyrics, and television, we can understand why seventy percent of our youth leave the church when they leave home. How necessary it becomes to keep God's words and commands in our hearts and in our children's hearts!

Twenty-one repetitions are needed to form a habit; therefore, from generation to generation, keep talking about your miracles and keep recording "stones of remembrance!" Why? Because hearing about deliverances is a unifying force that builds the faith of future generations. ***In a crisis, God can and will do it again!***

----
*Small leather box containing Scripture verses

Heavenly Father, in the name of Jesus Your Son, we ask You to bring the "seed" of the righteous in this nation back into Your Kingdom.

"Nevertheless, when the Son of Man comes, will He really find faith on the earth? --Luke 18:8."

"...In the future, when your children
ask you, 'What do these stones mean?'
tell them that the flow
of the Jordan was cut off
before the ark of the covenant
of the Lord. When it crossed
the Jordan, the waters
of the Jordan were cut off.
These stones are to be a memorial
to the people of Israel forever."
--Joshua 4:2-7

"By Faith They Overcame!"

"I could go on and on, but I've run out of time. There are so many more—Gideon, Barak, Samson, Jephthah, David, Samuel, the prophets.... Through acts of faith, they toppled kingdoms, made justice work, took the promises for themselves. They were protected from lions, fires, and sword thrusts, turned disadvantage to advantage, won battles, routed alien armies. Women received their loved ones back from the dead. There were those who, under torture, refused to give in and go free, preferring something better: resurrection. Others braved abuse and whips, and, yes, chains and dungeons. We have stories of those who were stoned, sawed in two, murdered in cold blood; stories of vagrants wandering the earth in animal skins, homeless, friendless, powerless—the world didn't deserve them!—making their way as best they could on the cruel edges of the world.

"Not one of these people, even though their lives of faith were exemplary, got their hands on what was promised. God had a better plan for us: that their faith and our faith would come together to make one completed whole, their lives of faith not complete apart from ours." --Hebrews 11:32-40 (THE MESSAGE—The Bible in Contemporary Language, Eugene H. Peterson, NAVPRESS, Colorado Springs, Colorado)

"And they overcame him [the devil]
by the blood of the Lamb
and by the word
of their testimony,...."
--Revelation 12:11

315

Printed in the United States
75860LV00004B/1-90

9 781425 947897